KU-005-715

The Architect and the British Country House
1620–1920

John Harris
The Architect and the British Country House
1620—1920

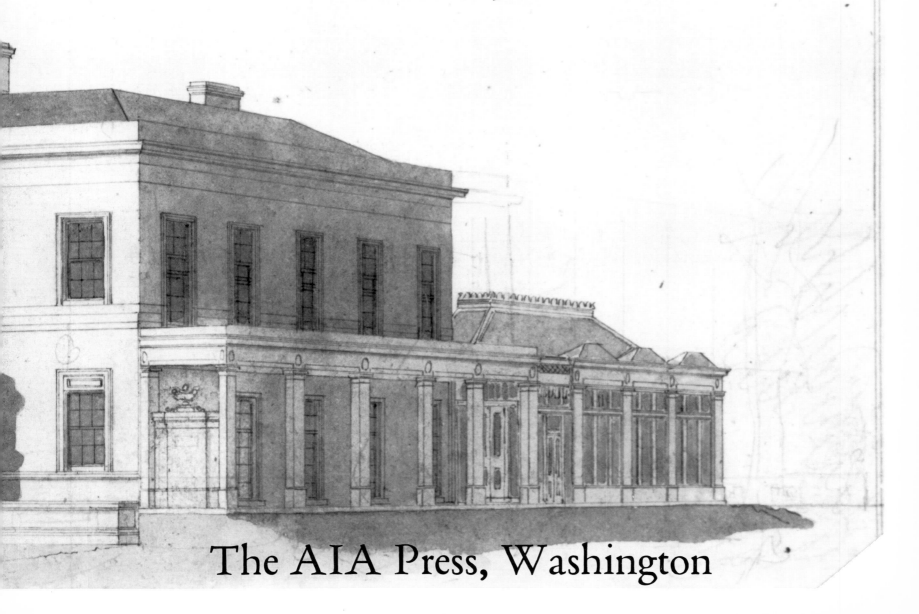

The AIA Press, Washington

The Exhibition was made possible by generous contributions from Paul Mellon, Hon. AIA, and Leo A. Daly, AIA and Mrs. Daly.
The Publication of this Catalogue was assisted by the Leo Daly Memorial Catalogue Fund of the American Institute of Architects Foundation

For Jane

Published in the United States of America by the American Institute of Architects Foundation, New York Avenue N.W., Washington D.C., U.S.A.
Copyright © The American Institute of Architects Foundation, 1985
First published 1985 by Trefoil Books and the American Institute of Architects Foundation

All rights reserved. No part of this publication may be reproduced, stored in any retrieval system, or transmitted in any form or by any means, without the prior permission in writing of the publishers.

ISBN 0-913962-75-9

Design & production by Conway Lloyd Morgan & Elizabeth van Amerongen
Set in Monophoto Poliphilus & printed by BAS Printers Ltd, Over Wallop.
Colour origination by Colorlito, Milan
Colour printed by Jolly & Barber Ltd, Rugby
Bound by Paperback Binders, Abingdon
Jacket printed by Shelley Press

Published on the occasion of the exhibition *The Architect and the British Country House*, at the Octagon, Washington, D.C., in November 1985.

Front cover illustration: Anthony Salvin's design for Scotney Castle, Kent. *See catalogue no 67.*

The Octagon Museum of the American Institute of Architects Foundation is pleased to present this exhibition and catalogue, *The Architect and the British Country House, 1620–1920*, which describes the development of British country house design. The exhibition complements the National Gallery of Art's exhibition *The Treasure Houses of Britain: Five Hundred Years of Patronage and Art Collecting* which features decorative arts and paintings displayed in country houses.

The Architect and the British Country House is the result of the successful collaboration of The American Institute of Architects Foundation and the Royal Institute of British Architects, whose renowned Drawings Collection formed the basis of the exhibition. A number of additional institutions and individuals have generously loaned works from their collections; we are appreciative.

At the Royal Institute of British Architects, we thank John Harris, the distinguished Curator of the Drawings Collection, who as Guest Curator shaped the exhibition and wrote the catalogue. Margaret Richardson, formerly Deputy Curator of the Drawings Collection and now Assistant Curator of Sir John Soane's Museum, reviewed the manuscript. Jane Preger, Exhibitions Specialist, patiently facilitated many details involving the conservation and transportation of the drawings.

At The American Institute of Architects Mary C. Means, President of The American Institute of Architects Foundation, recognized the importance of *The Architect and the British Country House* and saw that the Foundation's resources were devoted to it. The Director of The Octagon Museum, Susan R. Stein, organized the exhibition and publication. She was efficiently assisted by Judith S. Schultz, Assistant Curator of Exhibitions. The AIA Press, headed by James P. Cramer, worked closely with Trefoil Books to publish the catalogue.

The Architect and the British Country House would not have been possible without the generous contributions of Paul Mellon, HON. AIA, and Leo A. Daly, AIA and Mrs. Daly. We are grateful to them.

John A. Busby, Jr., FAIA
Chairman, Board of Directors
The American Institute of Architects Foundation

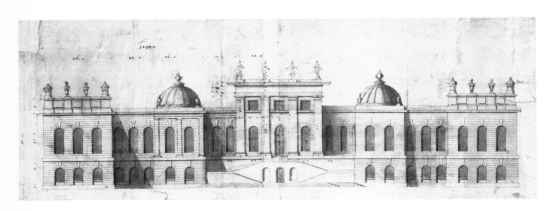

Contents

Not far from the American Institute of Architects' lovely Octagon in Washington, the National Gallery of Art are holding their *Treasure Houses of Britain* exhibition. As it were, the A.I.A. is all about the container and theirs what it contains. Of course, the N.G.A. is all glitter and gold and in contrast this show must appear drab. My original task was to display in one exhibition the architectural development of the British country house from about 1540 to 1920. To accomplish this in less than 100 drawings was impossible. Because designs for houses before 1580 are excessively rare I have begun the exhibition with Inigo Jones at 1620 and I end with Gordon Selfridge's castle, still being drawn out in 1920 but never built. I say 'British', but I really mean English, although I have introduced some decisive Scottish examples. Again, space prohibits showing the complex progress of Scottish country house design: a task that would have been made especially more difficult by the rarity of 17th century drawings. Throughout the exhibition a characteristic interior design of the period accompanies the exterior elevation, but this still does not take into account the planning of the house or the way furnishing and decoration were so often part of the same initiative. I have tried to make amends for some of these deficiences by departing in the catalogue from the usual format of image and catalogue description. Each exhibit is treated to a double-page spread, with the exhibit on the right-hand page and on the other its entry, plus one or more related images identified by the exhibit number plus a lower case letter *a*, *b*, or *c*. This enables me to offer a plan or perhaps a photograph of the house as built, or some image relevant to the architect, period or style. Prefacing the catalogue is an introduction with more than one hundred illustrations of many designs that could not be included in the exhibition, thus also helping to project a better visual understanding of the evolution of a building type that in Britain was far more varied and eclectic than in any other country.

There are many that I would like to thank for encouragement and help in the preparation of this exhibition and its accompanying book. First and foremost there are those lenders who have kindly agreed for their works to be shown:—
the Warden and Fellows of All Souls, Oxford, and Peter Lewis, Esq; the Viscount Coke, the Trustees of the Holkham Estate and Mr F. C. Jolly; the Duke of Devonshire, the Trustees of the Chatsworth Settlement and Peter Davy, Esq; Elvetham Hall Ltd. and Mr J. C. Holland; Bernard Pardoe, Esq; the Earl of Roseberry and Midlothian; the Viscount Scarsdale, the Trustees of the Kedleston Estate Trusts and Mr P. R. Snowden; the Victoria and Albert Museum and Dr Michael Kaufmann; the Yale Center for British Art and Duncan Robinson, Esq; and those lenders who prefer to remain anonymous.

I would also like to thank Finch Allibone, Miss Catherine Cruft, Mr Leslie Harris, Jill Lever, James Miller, Margaret Richardson, Alistair Rowan, Christopher White, and Professor John Wilton-Ely, as well as Charlotte Podrio for her conservation, repair and mounting of the drawings, and Geremy Butler for his photography.

I owe a debt of gratitude to Susan Stein for her co-operation and encouragement, and to her assistant Judith Schultz, as also to Jane Preger for her able organisation in London, and finally, and not least, to Conway Lloyd Morgan, my publisher.

John Harris, Portman Square, London, September 1985

Introduction

The visitor to the countryside of Britain today may be unaware that the decayed park wall and an entrance lodge now converted into a weekend 'house in the country' is all that is left of a great country house. It is difficult for him to realise that the country house was once the centre of a way of life to which nearly all the lands of England outside of the towns were subject. The nature of this way of life is often made clearer in parish churches, which contain in their memorials reminders of the vicissitudes of families, often in each church of several families all owning estates of varying acreages. In the same church there may be a monument to a duke and a squire, the latter enjoying a respectful but subservient relationship to his grander neighbour. Parish was linked to parish through family possession, patronage and marriage, and with many of the ducal territories a power structure would exist through many counties. This pattern of power is nowhere better demonstrated than in the pages of J. Bateman's *The Great Landowners of Great Britain and Ireland*, 1876. In brief, the country house is much more than the popular notion of a grand building in the countryside. It is, or rather was in the context of history, a means of organizing power (thus have they been called power houses) with a complex and cellular structure more or less self-supporting and often physically shut-off from the surrounding country by a park wall.

These great houses on their vast estates were in fact no more than a secular expression of the religious monasteries that had proliferated until Henry VIII dissolved them in the 1540s. They were then either demolished or partly demolished, usually for their materials, and sold or transferred to courtiers who converted them to secular use as domestic accommodation. In Mediaeval England there had been no country houses as we know them; only religious foundations, castles and fortified houses. Except in the Border country adjoining Scotland, by 1540 settlement and security were making the castle obsolete, and even earlier than this great brick towers such as Tattershall in Lincolnshire, about 1445, or even the symmetrically-planned brick Herstmonceux Castle in Sussex (1), about 1440, were hardly designed to resist prolonged assault. By about 1500 the powerful barons who had needed private castles for their own gain and protection were becoming courtiers, both politically and financially dependent upon the Crown. This dependence led

1. Herstmonceux Castle, Sussex
Drawing for the engraving by S. & N. Buck, 1737

the barons to emulate the royal establishments in matters of servants and retainers and in the heirarchical structure that went therewith, and for this most of the barons' castles, sometimes intended to be no more than a shelter for a disorderly rabble, were unfitted. By the mid-sixteenth century a plan of ordered accommodation, in circumstances that were peaceful rather than belligerent, was required. The qualities of a soldier were now subservient to those of a courtier. From this point on it became possible to develop the concept of an estate with a comfortable country house as its centre of operations. From the 1540s until the Agricultural Depression began in 1873, the house on its estate was a working system that appeared inviolate and everlasting.

In a sense the order that had entered the lives of landowners now influenced planning. Order demands a certain balance and symmetry began to affect the design of elevations. The Mediaeval house was asymmetrical because it had evolved from use and function, not from design. (It would take another 250 years before the picturesque qualities of a Mediaeval country house were again appreciated. Indeed, if a Mediaeval country house survived until 1800, as did Ashton Court, Somerset (2), that survival was often because of those very qualities of asymmetry and variation then so appreciated. Rather it was the great classical houses that fell to the onslaught of the Picturesque improvers.)

The new status, role and image of the Tudor courtier after

2. Ashton Court, Somerset
Watercolour by John Chessell Buckler, 1825

3. Loseley, Surrey
The garden front
Country Life

the Dissolution brought with it the need for education. Learning had been shut up in the monasteries, not the castles, and only in the matter of the arts of fortification were qualities of design expressed in castles. The new courtiers who were acquiring a taste for the classics along with a classical education gradually became sensitive to Renaissance principles of symmetry and balance, and began to incorporate Italian Renaissance, or Franco-Italian Renaissance ornament and decoration into design. It is still unclear whether many Tudor courtiers read their Vitruvius. Those editions that have been recorded in Tudor libraries may have been there simply because Vitruvius was a standard Latin text. Tudor builders preferred illustrated works, hence the popularity of Sebastiano Serlio's *Libri*, of which parts four and three were first published in Venice in 1537 and 1540, and parts one and two in 1545 when Serlio was working for the French court. Part five followed in 1547 and part six the *Libro Estraordinario*, containing useful designs for doors and gates in 1551. Only in 1566 were these conveniently collected together in a single volume. There were other treatises, but it is unclear just how much, for example, the works by Labacco of 1552, Cataneo of 1554, the first edition of Vignola's orders in 1556, and Palladio's celebrated *Quattro Libri* of 1570, were used by the Tudors. They preferred northern

publications, of Flemish or French origin and were more in sympathy with such French books as Du Cerceau's *Livre d'Architectura* of 1559 and *Les Plus Excellents Bastiments* of 1576 and of Philibert de l'Orme's *Nouvelles Inventions* of 1561 and *Les Premier Tome d'Architecture* of 1568.

In the Tudor age an architect in the modern sense did not exist. The act of design was still basically unchanged from the activity of the itinerant masons of the cathedrals. The freemasons might produce what was called a 'platt' or plan and an 'upright' or elevation, always drawn with an imperfect understanding of perspective and rarely with applied wash. More likely the mason would only be an executive of the ideas and wishes of his courtly employer, for only the courtier possessed a critical faculty or judgement in design. So many of our Tudor, Elizabethan and Jacobean mansions were conceived from the owner's research in his architectural pattern books, or observation of what his friends and peers were doing. Much was built empirically, so that a plan might be begun and discontinued, a facade erected and then partly demolished or modified. The extent of any intervention by the owner in the design of his house cannot always be judged, for the documents to prove such intervention rarely survive. However, there is no need to disbelieve that this 'amateur intervention' between about 1550 and 1620 was just as decisive then, as it would be in the eighteenth century.

The quest for symmetry was not a straight-forward accomplishment. A house might appear with balanced wings as Loseley, Surrey (3) in 1561 but with symmetry and balance of fenestration still lacking in the centre. There is some evidence that the imposition of a grid system of surrounding formal gardens often led to a desire to match up the bays and divisions of the elevation to the garden, as had occured on the south front of Haddon Hall in Derbyshire about 1600 (4). Perfectly symmetrical plans on all fronts were only achieved during the reign of Queen Elizabeth when her courtiers were building their so-called Prodigy Houses.

The most original house of this time was Longleat in Wiltshire, (5) representing Sir John Thynne's search for perfection. It matters not that Longleat developed with stops and starts, only that by 1572 the present block-like four-sided palace was determined as a design by Robert Smythson, the genius of the Tudor Renaissance who had absorbed his architectural knowledge from his master and mentor Thynne. It represents the High Renaissance of Elizabethan architecture and could be called England's first contribution since the English Gothic to North European architecture. Longleat was a fuse for the explosion of astonishing prodigy houses throughout the country, many of them built to honour, please and house the Queen, regardless of expense, on her progresses around her kingdom.

Longleat was Smythson's testing ground, and proof of his genius is that even then he had no peer among Elizabethan designers as a draughtsman, as his design for the Longleat window proves (6). This single drawing is as important in the history of architectural draughtsmanship in England as is Longleat as a building. Smythson would go on to design and build at least half-a-dozen magisterial houses, including Hardwick Hall, Derbyshire, and Worksop Manor, Nottinghamshire. Wollaton, Nottinghamshire (7) built for Sir Francis Willoughby in 1580 encapsulates Smythson's veneration for Serlio as a paper source, both for details of the orders and designs for chimney pieces. Taking his cue from Serlio, Smythson placed the Great Hall squarely in the centre of the house, and drew it up and out of the body for a full three storeys as a clerestoried tower. If this was a remarkable and innovative achievement, so was the garden, locked-in to the elevations in perfect unity (8) as Smythson's design shows. Even the great Nicholas Hawksmoor had to confess in 1731 that Wollaton contained 'some true strokes of architecture'.

If we single out one achievement on Smythson's part it would surely be his handling of the cubic mass, working up from his

4. Haddon Hall, Derbyshire
The garden front from the terrace
Country Life

5. Longleat, Wiltshire
The garden front
Country Life

6. *Robert Smythson*
Design for a window at Longleat
RIBA

7. *Robert Smythson*
Wollaton Hall, Northamptonshire
The entrance front
National Monuments Record

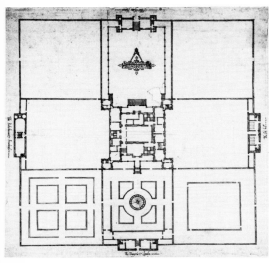

8. *Robert Smythson*
Wollaton Hall
Ground floor plan
RIBA

10. Burghley, Northamptonshire
The garden front
Country Life

9.*Robert Smythson*
Hardwick Hall
The New Hall
National Monuments Record

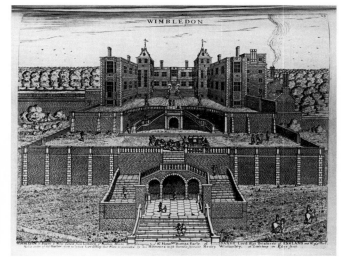

11. Wimbledon House, Surrey
Engraving by Henry Winstanley, 1678

plan with squares and rectangles, with or without towers or pavilions at the angles. Hardwick Hall (9), designed for Bess of Hardwick from 1590 is proof of this. The massing of fronts, the tiers of window bays, the romantic towers and broken skylines, are what we remember most of Elizabethan houses. Lord Burghley's vast house (10) at Burghley in Northampton-shire, built expressly 'for the Quene and her greate traine' is the ideal Prodigy house, and nowhere else in England is there a house with a roof-scape so full of architectural wonder.

It was not surprising that Lord Burghley's son Sir Thomas Cecil should also have built on a grand scale. His first contribu-tion to the progress of planning was his Wimbledon House in Surrey begun in 1588 (11), one of the first houses in the form of a capital H, although Wimbledon was not a true H as the wings on one front were not fully pulled out. The H-plan and its variations established a type that would serve for the next century and a half. At Wimbledon the main entrance was in the centre of the cross-wing into a traditional screens passage and thus from there, by means of a right-angle turn, into the

12. Rushbrooke Hall, Suffolk
The entrance front
National Monuments Record

13. Bramshill, Hampshire
The entrance front
National Monuments Record

Great Hall. A house such as Rushbrooke Hall in Suffolk (12) showed the type perhaps ten years later. Bramshill in Hampshire (13), Lord Zouche's great mansion of 1605 displays the Elizabethan and Jacobean architect's fancy at building-up fantastic centre-pieces. Already Smythson at Hardwick had found in the pages of his Palladio the idea of placing the hall across the stroke in the centre of his plan. By 1607 at Charlton House, Kent, the hall would be entered axially, with only a porch-vestibule acting as a screen to the hall proper. Charlton only requires the hall to be divided transversely into two to achieve an approximation of what architects after about 1640 would call the 'double pile', the standard plan form for the years 1640 to 1750. Since Mediaeval times the hall had served as the social centre of the house, and from late Mediaeval times it was so used in conjunction with the great chamber on the first floor and then with the long gallery. Out of high chambers and parlours would emerge the modern notions of drawing- and dining-rooms, with the hall relegated to an entrance place. Only in the nineteenth century would the hall once more be used for social gatherings or for billiards. In the greater houses the long gallery remained a constant feature, although their function in the eighteenth century would be as much a setting for displays of artistic possessions and particularly sculpture, as for that of exercise.

In the 1570s part of Burghley the staircase was a stone-vaulted spiral after a French model, but this was special, and most

Elizabethan stairs were simple spirals or were square, the flights arranged around a square well. Only after about 1590 when great advances had been made in joinery construction was more ingenuity displayed (14) in complex arrangements of flights, with the newels used to display carved figure sculpture. Many of these staircases as at Hatfield or Knole were containers providing a claustrophobic concentration of painting and wood carving. Similarly the rich plaster ceilings of the parlours (15) would provide a canopy of pendants or complex strapwork, and always the chimney-piece became a focus of attention as well as expense.

When Queen Elizabeth died in 1603, James the First's accession introduced the Jacobean age. In the same year the Earl of Suffolk began a vast mansion at Audley End in Essex (16), which, even before it was finished, was redundant. The age of Prodigy houses had passed. Even as Audley End's foundations were being laid, a painter—Inigo Jones—and his entourage were hurrying home from Italy to attend the new court. A Renaissance in the true sense of that word was soon to begin.

14. Staircase at Aston Hall, Warwickshire
From C.J. Richardson, *Studies from Old English Mansions*, 1848

15. The Carved Parlour, Crewe Hall, Cheshire
From C.J. Richardson, *Studies from Old English Mansions*, 1842

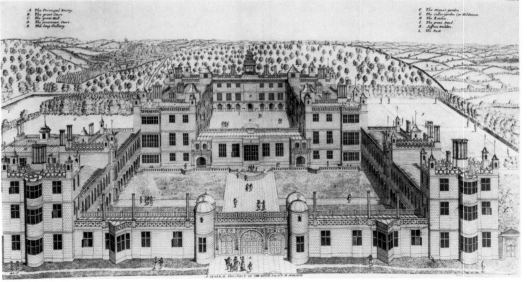

16. Audley End, Essex
The entrance front
National Monuments Record

INTRODUCTION

HOUSES OF THE JACOBEAN AND FIRST STUART COURTS: 1620–1640

For all that we may glory in 'Hardwick Hall more window than wall' and extoll the dramatic effects achieved in such houses, we should not forget that Palladio had been dead for more than ten years by the time it had been begun. Even if Elizabethan 'surveyors' such as Smythson and John Thorpe had access to Palladio's work, it remained a mystery to them, and the purity of its classical architecture was not only misunderstood, but was generally unwelcome in an age that revered chivalry and pageantry, adopted romantic postures, and whose *mise-en-scène* was the fantasy of the Royal Progress. We could not imagine a Palladian villa being built in the English Elizabethan countryside.

There is a tendency to pass unfavourable judgement on Elizabethan architecture by comparing it to Italian Renaissance architecture. It is fairer to set the English achievement in the context of the north European Renaissance of Flanders, North

Germany and Denmark. The criterion that identifies an Inigo Jones or any able Renaissance architect is his ability to think of a building inside-out, so that, for example, the windows of an elevation would fit the rooms inside symmetrically. So often, even with a Hardwick, this matching does not always occur, for the likes of Smythson drew the elevation first and thought of the rooms afterwards. The gradual appreciation of order and rationality that began to affect country house design was concurrent with the introduction of Italianate models. But it needs to be said at once that Inigo Jones cannot be used as a measure of the average in design after 1620, for his involvement was always exceptional, and reserved for the Royal family or for courtiers close to Charles I. We may wonder at the genius and invention of his design for the Prince's Lodging at Newmarket of 1619 (17) that seems to prophesy everything about the country house after 1660 , or observe how his 'Lord Maltravers' design of about 1638 (18) or the 'Villa' design, (1) some twenty years before, spells out so much of the neo-Palladian villa in the coming century, but none of this belonged to the mainstream of

17. *Inigo Jones*
Prince's lodging, Newmarket
Elevation
RIBA

18. *Inigo Jones*
Adaptation of the 'Lord Maltravers' design
Worcester College, Oxford

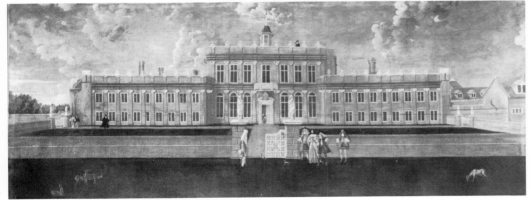

19. *Issac de Caus*
Woburn, Bedfordshire
Painted by Randolph Schwabe after Sir Jonas
Moore's plan.
Country Life

20. Denham Place, Buckinghamshire
View of the entrance front, before 1674, by
Peter Hartover

21. Wisbech Castle, Cambridgeshire
Anonymous painting of the castle
Wisbech and Fenland Museum

early seventeenth-century country house endeavour. When a courtier like the Earl of Bedford required the modernisation of his country house (19) at Woburn in Bedfordshire, instead of employing Jones, who had designed Covent Garden for him, he was content with Isaac de Caus: and his fenestration there betrays his subordinate status.

Since Wimbledon progress had been made upon developing more compactly the H, U and square or oblong block plans. Since the end of the sixteenth century straight-forward triangular gables had developed more curvaceous forms, and by 1620 they could be pedimented, in response to gable-types from Flanders and Northern Europe. Jones himself may have introduced the so-called Netherlandish gable to London and a house such as the exceptional Raynham Hall, Norfolk (4) draws directly upon this source .

Since 1580 the building trades had vastly improved, especially the crafts of joinery and brickwork. Indeed, someone travelling through the Home Counties in the 1620s would be particularly impressed with the emergence of brick houses, built for bankers and merchants with City connections and reflecting the crafts of the City Companies' craftsmen. If many of these houses were robust in style they were crude in detail, though such houses are the source for that idiosyncratic fashion, termed Artisan Mannerism, which developed and flourished during the Commmonwealth. Such a style might be epitomised by Denham Place, Buckinghamshire (20) built for Sir William Bowyer in the 1650s, or Wisbech Castle, Cambridgeshire (21), built for John Thurloe in 1658. The comparison between these and a house such as Chevening in Kent, built before 1630 (22) is a telling one. Chevening is one of the few houses that could be by Inigo Jones had he ever been inclined to design country houses.

INTRODUCTION

first sitke chimny poos for oatlands
1636

2. Inigo Jones (1573-1652)
Oatlands Palace, Surrey.
Elevation
Pen and pencil (260 x 190)
See pages 78-79

11. Attributed to Edward Goudge (fl. 1680- about 1700)
Design for a Restoration period ceiling
Brown pen over pencil outline and some wash (355 x 245)
See pages 96-97

14. *Sir John Vanbrugh (1664-1736)*
& Nicholas Hawksmoor
Castle Howard, Yorkshire
Design for a new house
Elevation of entrance front
Pen and grey washes (360 x 1060)
See pages 102-103

17. *Nicholas Hawksmoor (c.1661-1736)*
Wotton House, Surrey
Design for a new house
Elevation of entrance front
Pen, pencil & wash (335 x 830)
See pages 108-109

ARCHITECTURAL SOCIETY INSTITUTE A.D. 1831.

26. *Richard Boyle, 3rd Earl of Burlington (1694-1753)* &
Henry Flitcroft (1697-1769)
Chiswick House, Middlesex
Design for the south or entrance front
Elevation, with scale Pen and wash (310 x 370)
See pages 126-127

24. *Colen Campbell (1676-1729)*
Mereworth Castle, Kent
Preliminary design for the interior
Section, with scale
Pen and wash (330 x 465)
See pages 122-123

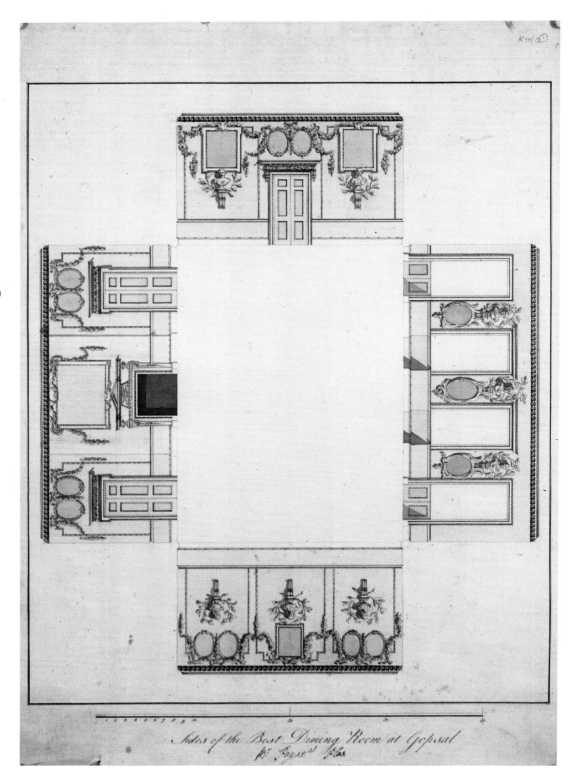

Sides of the Best Dining Room at Gopsal

Sanderson 1770

A Design for the Great Room at Kimberly in Norfolk

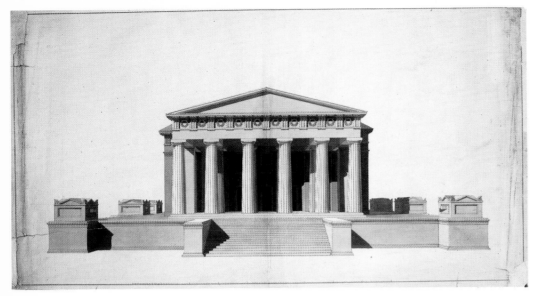

52. *William Wilkins (1778-1839)*
The Grange, Hampshire
Design for the east or portico front
Elevation in perspective
Pen and wash (330 x 585)
See pages 178-179

51. *Joseph Bonomi (1739-1808)*
Rosneath, Dunbartonshire
Design for a new house
Perspective
Pen and watercolour (620 x 990)
See pages 176-177

If other houses of the quality of Chevening were built, they remain unrecorded. It is almost possible to suggest that, with the exception of John Webb, all of Jones's subordinates built in a subordinate style. The other exception may be Edward Carter, whose design for Easthampstead Lodge (23) in Berkshire, made soon after 1626, is remarkable, and entitles him to be considered as second only to Jones. The plan is based upon Rubens's *Palazzi di Genova*, published in 1622, a reminder that the *Palazzi* was a source for the double-pile plan. Chevening prepares the way for a type of house made into a canon by Sir Roger Pratt during the Commonwealth. With a few notable exceptions, courtly building ceased during Cromwell's reign, and subordinate or artisan building flourished. This was a time for courtiers who had not fled into exile to keep a low profile.

One exception was Coleshill in Berkshire, (24) built for Sir George Pratt by his 'cousin' Sir Roger Pratt from 1650. It may claim to be the most considered house of the century, the result of years of musings by a remarkable gentleman-amateur on architecture in France and Italy as well as upon Jones's buildings. Pratt gave his novel house two storeys of equal importance, spacing the windows three-three-three with the middle two more widely spaced in recognition of the fact that behind them was a two-storey hall on one front and the great parlour with dining chamber over on the other. Pratt split his double-pile plan to right and left of the hall by spine corridoors, and his was the innovative decision to place the stairs within the hall, rising from each side to a gallery. Roof, dormer windows, chimney stacks and balustraded platform with cupola were all scrupulously proportioned. Rarely can one call a house perfect, but Coleshill was perfection, even if, as with a design by Jones, there are identifiable sources. Houses such as Chevening had already pioneered the balustraded roof platform, but Pratt, as had Jones, demonstrated his mastery and genius by destroying his sources in the process of assimilation. Its date so early in the Protectorate makes Coleshill so special, for not until the Restoration did Pratt get the opportunity to build again, and in the space of two years he achieved a multiple success by designing three houses, all modifications or amplifications of the Coleshill style. In 1663 he began Kingston Lacy, Dorset (25) and Horseheath, Cambridgeshire, and in 1664 his greatest house, Clarendon House

22. Chevening, Kent Drawing from a land survey

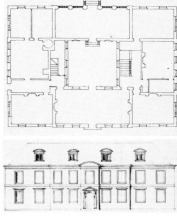

23. *Edward Carter*
Easthampstead Lodge, Berkshire
Berkshire Record Office

24. *Sir Roger Pratt*
Coleshill, Berkshire

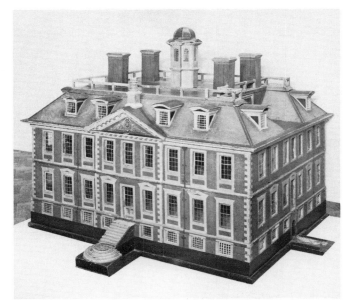

26. Melton Constable, Norfolk
Model of the house
Norwich Museums Committee

27. Belton House, Lincolnshire The entrance
front
Country Life

in Piccadilly, which was immensely influential by virtue of its situation. All three houses were astylar and all had a hipped roof finished off with a platform and cupola. The marked difference from Coleshill was the division of the bays into 3-3-3, with the middle three given prominence by being advanced under a pediment. Clarendon House was much the largest, a Kingston Lacy with wings, and of H-plan. The type exercised a magnetic influence, and varieties exist by the dozen, some being by Wren's associate Robert Hooke. For example, Melton Constable, Norfolk (26), about 1680, is a child of Kingston Lacy, as Belton House, Lincolnshire, 1684, (27) is of Clarendon House.

Reflecting upon country house design during the Royal Surveyorship of Inigo Jones, it does seem unusual that Jones never built a country house, as Pratt and his successors were to do. Part of the reason may possibly be Jones's disinclination to spend the time needed in travelling to the country and supervising work. So, however splendid the south front of Wilton may be, we must now accept that it was built by Isaac de Caus, from the late 1630s, and rehabilitated after fire by John Webb from 1649. But Jones's influence was probably more directly felt in matters of interior decoration, especially in the design of chimney-pieces (2), for there can be little argument

25. *Sir Roger Pratt*
Kingston Lacy, Dorset
North elevation
National Trust

INTRODUCTION

that Jones was incomparably the best chimney-piece designer in Northern Europe. He was also responsible for a revolution in the proportion of rooms, as if Vitruvian man was casting his shadow over Jacobean spaces. In that often parts can be better grasped than the whole, so Jones's subordinates often selected those parts of his interiors that attracted them, although they never did understand that the grammar of his decoration was frequently based upon Palladio's fourth book, that devoted to Roman antiquity. It was Jones who introduced to the English interior what the Italians called a *conca di volta* or a coved ceiling.

In all these matters John Webb was the lonely exception to a general rule of misunderstanding or ignorance of Jones's methods. Webb was Jones's personal assistant from 1627 until Jones died in 1652. Webb designed at Wilton the only surviving suite of state rooms of the kind that Jones had designed for his royal palaces. Yet he got little credit: by 1700 he had beeen forgotten, and the myth established that every building by Webb was by Jones. By 1650 he was the tainted assistant of the Royalist Jones, and clearly at a disadvantage. Although he obtained a growing number of commissions for country house alterations, most were for Cromwellians or middle-of-the-road men. When the Restoration came in 1660 he was the obvious and right successor to Jones as Surveyor of the Royal Works, but the climate had already changed, and the Palladianism of Jones was already old-fashioned. Despite this, Webb built two of the most influential country houses of the whole century: Gunnersbury House, Middlesex, (28) and Amesbury House, Wiltshire (29) both building by 1658, and therefore just pre-Restoration. It was as if Jones had returned from the grave and become a country house architect, for these two houses represent the apotheosis of the Jonesian canon of design, if such had ever existed. Both draw upon Jones and Palladio. Gunnersbury is a proper villa paying homage to the Queen's House and Newmarket designs and with a highly original plan, containing a columnar undercroft cut right throughout the house · from under the portico. At Amesbury the plan is based upon that of Palladio's Villa Godi, and there was not to be a more magnificent portico until Campbell's at Wanstead in 1713. But neither of these houses had any influence upon contemporary design, and when they were rediscovered by the neo-Palladians they were thought to have been masterworks by Jones. Both, therefore, are isolated episodes in the evolution of the country house after 1660.

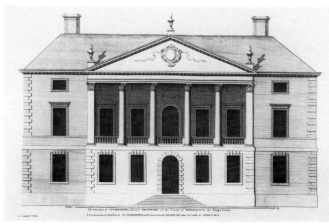

28. *John Webb*
Gunnersbury House, Middlesex
From *Vitruvius Britannicus*

29. *John Webb*
Amesbury House, Wiltshire
Measured drawing by Wyatt Papworth, 1840, from an earlier drawing
RIBA

The Restoration and Williamite House: 1660 to 1700

What came after the Restoration has often been signalled as a culture superior to that of the previous decade. But any decade with Coleshill, Gunnersbury and Amesbury to its credit is a notable one, and it must not be thought that Continental influences had been banished during the Proctectorate, which was rather a time for introspection, and the quiet repair and consolidation of estates. The Artisan-Mannerist style can be followed through to the 1670s, and by 1660 Pratt had shown what would become the quintessential English house: characteristic of which, and one of the most beautiful, is Hooke's Ramsbury, Wiltshire. Change would come from the Continent, for the Royal family and their courtiers in exile had become conditioned to French and Dutch fashions, and it was natural that they should want to introduce some of these to England. The significant change in country house design is that for the first time it is possible to say that a house is in the French or Dutch style.

Hugh May, that 'very ingenious man' as Pepys called him, had spent at least four years in Holland and had also made a study of French architecture. His brick Eltham Lodge, Kent built for Sir John Shaw in 1664 is decidedly Dutch, and with Berkeley House, Piccadilly, for Lord Berkeley in 1665, he built a house as influential as its neighbour Clarendon House. Not only does Berkeley House appear to have conformed to the brick and stone-coigned, hipped-roofed, Pratt type, but in addition it possessed quadrant colonnades breaking forward to offices enclosing the courtyard. There is also evidence that its plan was developed from Coleshill's, with staircases set in spine corridors. May's other interesting house was Cassiobury, Hertfordshire, (30) built for the Earl of Essex in 1677. In all these houses there is both a novelty in planning and a new handling of spatial effects. Cassiobury possessed the first oval room in England, painted by Antonio Verrio. An oval painted room is a Baroque room, and at Cassiobury, as well as in the apartments that May was decorating in Windsor Castle, a new style emerges. Interiors have painted ceilings, usually with painted coves, or the ceilings may be of rich naturalistic plasterwork in the style of Edward Goudge, while walls are divided into bolection-framed panels for pictures, or overmantels for chimney-pieces are composed of highly naturalistic carved woodwork by Grinling Gibbons. As this new style was not Pratt's, it seeems likely to have been introduced by May himself. The high point of his work was St George's Hall and the Royal Chapel at Windsor, where we have a fictive style of painting, plasterwork and carving combined with spatially-exciting planning that elevates Windsor to a level of Baroque opulence not even matched by Versailles.

One other architect deserves to be singled out for his remarkable houses, few though they were. William Samwell was another gentleman-amateur who, like Pratt, could rise above the commonplace. His Eaton Hall, Cheshire, of 1675 (31) and Grange Park, Hampshire, perhaps about 1670, follow the Pratt formula, but the rythmn of Eaton's bays was 1-2-3-2-1 with the end bays breaking forward as pavilions containing cabinet

30. *Hugh May*
Cassiobury, Hertfordshire
From Knyff and Kipp, *Britannia Illustrata*, 1708

it may well be because it always was a village house standing right on the road. In that sense it is not a country house.

It is no dishonour to Wren to suggest that, like Jones, he was disinterested in the country house round. Country houses demanded the sort of supervision that involved much time and travel for a London-based architect, and it is not surprising that Wren with his multifarious commitments had no time for this. It could well be that he passed on many commissions to his colleagues, notably Robert Hooke, with whom he enjoyed a happy working relationship. Hooke may prove to have been a far more prolific country house architect than has so far been shown. As he designed Ramsbury in Wiltshire in about 1680, he may well have designed such related houses as Stanstead in

31. *William Samwell*
Eaton Hall, Cheshire
From *Vitruvius Britannicus*, II, 1717

32. Winslow Hall, Buckinghamshire
The garden front
Country Life

rooms in the angles. The Grange, Eaton, and Ashburnham House, Westminster, also attributed to him, exploit versions of voussoired openings in the French manner that endow Eaton in particular with a curious proto-Gibbsian look. All Sam-well's houses also appear to have possessed staircases of complex design: the one surviving at Ashburnham House might suggest that Samwell travelled to France sometime after 1656.

During the early nineteenth century the myth was created that every red-brick, stone-coigned house of any distinction— and many of none—was by Sir Christopher Wren. Even now his contribution to country house design is in fact a matter for speculation. Tring Manor House in Hertfordshire, built for Henry Guy and Winslow Hall, Buckinghamshire, (32) for William Lowndes have withstood the scrutiny of historians. The dating of Tring is in dispute, for although it was granted to Guy in 1669 it may not hae been built until about 1685. Not surprisingly—if it is the work of Wren, who was a scientist before he was an architect—Tring does not have any obvious parentage. It is unremarkable outside, and in the spacing of the windows and the oddly-placed niches not a little clumsy, but inside Wren showed great ingenuity in planning, even though it was unconventional. There are similarities, too, with Easton Neston. Winslow is something quite different and its accounts are dated 1699. It relies almost entirely for its effect upon the subtle proportion of window to wall and the immaculate quality of the bricks and brickwork. It looks particulary urban, and

Sussex of 1686 (33), whose attribution to William Talman is unconvincing; but whoever the architect, these houses typify the best of this sort of English house. At the same time, Hooke was also the architect of Montagu House in London, 1675 and Ragley Hall in Warwickshire, 1679 (34), both in a French style and a reminder that there was a small group of houses in England built either by French architects, or strongly dependent upon French sources. There was Boughton House, Northamptonshire, building from 1683, Petworth House, Sussex, from 1688, which almost certainly involved the design skills of Daniel Marot, and Bretby, that unsung house in Derbyshire (35), an enlargement, from the late 1660s, of a Jacobean house of 1610 with a huge pavilioned cross-wing of about 1670, surely by an architect of the Le Vau school, if not by Louis Le Vau himself. Indeed its central pavilion is a domestic version of Le Vau's Collège des Quatre Nations of 1662.

The one country house architect in England whose work consistently reveals his reliance upon French engraved sources is William Talman. Between about 1680 and 1715 he was involved in no less than twenty country houses, and can claim to be the chief country house architect of the Williamite Court. As Comptroller of the Royal Works he seems to have been favoured by William III over Wren, and when the king died in 1702 Talman fell from favour and lost his royal appointments. His work can be seen as a bridge between the school of Pratt, May and Samwell and that of Vanbrugh and Hawksmoor, and there is circumstanial evidence that he learnt much from a study of May's work. Like Pratt and Samwell he was a

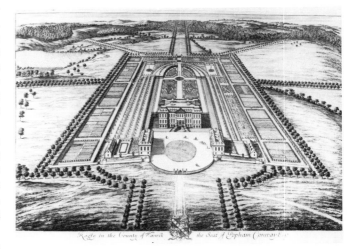

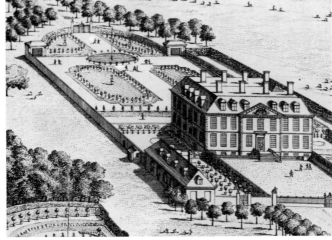

33. *Robert Hooke*
Stanstead, Sussex

34. *Robert Hooke*
Ragley Hall, Warwickshire
From Knyff and Kipp, *Britannia Illustrata*, 1708

35. Bretby, Derbyshire
From Knyff and Kipp, *Britannia Illustrata*, 1708

INTRODUCTION

gentleman-amateur who acted profesionally, and his amateur approach to architecture made him receptive to innovation and new ideas, although many of his designs incorporate invention in an ill-digested way. His architectural library of books, prints and drawings was possibly the largest in the world and from this source his designs and buildings are always enriched with some idiosyncracy. In planning, elevation and decoration, his work always produced something novel, as a single design for an unknown country house (36) suffices to show. Both Eaton and Coleshill are called to pay tribute here, and the house looks forward to James Gibbs and the style of the *Book of Architecture* of 1728. With the great south front of Chatsworth in Derbyshire (37) he produced in 1687 what may be called the first Baroque front in England, behind which are suites of painted, carved and embellished apartments, developing the May-Verrio Windsor style. The same development was continued in his splendid series of painted apartments at Burghley House, Northamptonshire, from 1688. In retrospect Talman's work is the product of a man of ideas, and this is his importance in a period of transition. When Talman contested Castle Howard with Sir John Vanbrugh in 1698 and lost, he was forced to admit the supremacy of the new Baroque School of the Vanbrugh-Hawksmoor partnership.

THE BAROQUE COUNTRY HOUSE: 1700-1720

A simplistic definition of the Baroque would be the rough rather than the smooth, the ornamented rather than the unornamented, the complex rather than the simple, the advance and recess of planes rather than the flat surface. We have already suggested that around 1675 Hugh May had introduced a Baroque episode to English architecture with his fictive ensembles of apartments and complex, theatric stairs at Windsor, and at Cassiobury with his introduction of the first oval room. Strength, power and emphasis are the attributes of Talman's south front at Chatsworth, where for the first time in a country house the facades were spanned by a giant order, though John Webb had already used the giant order in a new way at the unfinished royal palace at Greenwich in 1664. Greenwich anticipates much in the Baroque to come: massiveness, chunky or blocked, rusti-

cated windows and an overall wall rustication. Apart from Chatsworth the Baroque becomes more evident in certain aspects of planning, notably the handling of the corridor, and in the use of columnar screens in rooms or halls. There was also more concern with spatial effect in the relationship of the main block to offices, which were often linked together by quadrant arcades or colonnades; the relative positioning of one to the other would become a critical factor.

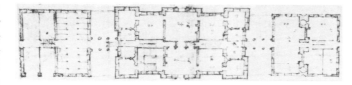

36. *William Talman*
Design for unknown house
The Warden and Fellows of All Souls, Oxford

37. *William Talman*
South front of Chatsworth

All this can be observed in Vanbrugh's first design for Castle Howard (14), that in matters of conception is a child of Greenwich. Nothing like it had been seen before in English architecture, and it took a man with experience in the theatre and breadth of imagination and mind to conceive it. For Castle Howard, and Blenheim Palace, Oxfordshire, (38/39) building from 1705, are expressed in a language quite alien to the Baroque of the rest of Europe. No other houses had developed what Hawks-

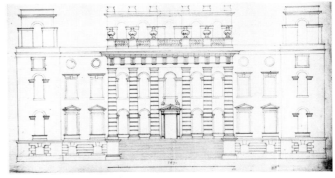

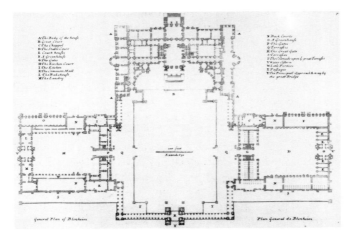

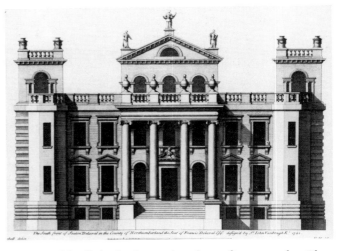

38. *Sir John Vanbrugh*
Blenheim Palace
From *Vitruvius Britannicus*, I, 1715

39. *Sir John Vanbrugh*
Blenheim Palace
Plan from *Vitruvius Britannicus*, I, 1715

40. *Sir John Vanbrugh*
Eastbury House, Dorset
From *Vitruvius Britannicus*, III, 1725

41. *Sir John Vanbrugh*
Seaton Delaval, Northumberland
From *Vitruvius Britannicus*, III, 1725

moor would call the 'eminences' or the roof-scape, and at Blenheim these are stated in appropriately martial tones. Because of their size both houses were never finished, and both were soon to become out-of-date. Vanbrugh would go on to design the huge Eastbury House, Dorset, in 1718 (40) and Seaton Delaval, Northumberland, (41) in 1720. Hawksmoor, an architect of the urban scene, would never command a country house practice, whereas Vanbrugh would continue to build numerous country houses and remodel old ones. All were astonishingly idiosyncratic, and frequently in a fortified or castle style (43)

INTRODUCTION

that owed much to the Board of Ordnance and to the fact that Vanbrugh, having been a soldier, enjoyed adopting military airs.

Because Vanbrugh's works were so personal, they exercised little influence as models for copying. But his influence was profound on the masons and craftsmen employed on his buildings, who all in some way became imbued with his style. This influence could be spread by regional factors, for the building of a house such as Eastbury, for example, might influence the style of other local buildings designed by provincial architects or builders, often because the contracting mason might well absorb something of Vanbrugh's style by association. In other cases an architect would make a deliberate examination of the works of a great or greater colleague and re-interpret this in a personal way. Such is the case with Thomas Archer who is another example of that peculiarly English phenomenon, the gentleman-amateur. He had studied continental architecture in the 1690s in Rome and returned to design a whole stream of houses all strongly tinctured with detail culled from Bernini, Borromini and the Late Roman Baroque. His was the curved north front of Chatsworth in 1704, the Roman-style palace of Heythrop, Oxfordshire in 1707 (43), Roehampton House, Surrey with its huge broken pediment of 1710, and Chettle House, Dorset, (44) with its curved angles and echoes of Eastbury, in 1711. All these reveal an intelligent study of Vanbrugh and of Williamite architecture, onto which he grafted his Roman Baroque details: eared and lugged corners, tapered pilasters, broken and reversed pediments, concavo-convex walls to entrances and courts. Archer's houses are consistently interesting, as indelibly stamped with his own style as those of Vanbrugh.

42. *Sir John Vanbrugh*
Vanbrugh Castle
Drawn by T.C. Donaldson, 1833
RIBA

43. *Thomas Archer*
Heythrop House, Oxfordshire
From a survey by Thomas Bainbridge, 1790
Private collection

INTRODUCTION

33

As a gentleman he obviously required a contracting mason and builder, and so we find the brothers Francis and William Smith of Warwick building Heythrop, and coming under the influence of Archer's style. Thus the Smiths would exploit the use of giant orders or emphatically-framed windows. They favoured the block-like house, typically nine bays wide and three storeys high, which might be framed with giant pilasters, or they might, as at Wingerworth Hall, Derbyshire, in 1726 (46) create an astylar elevation of rows of finely-cut windows with big keystones, capped with a balustraded and flat roof. Their interiors were always fine examples of good masonry and joinery, and their halls were often framed with giant pilasters (45). The Smiths are the contemporary equivalent in the provinces of what can be described in London as the 'School of Baroque Compromise', a style perfectly encapsulated by James Gibbs's *Book of Architecture* of 1728, and which developed as an alternative style to Neo-Palladianism; a school of compromise in that it was neither an extreme Baroque nor an extreme neo-Palladian style.

This can also be seen in the work of John James, who wrote to the Duke of Buckingham in 1711 that 'the Beautys of Archi-

44. *Thomas Archer*
Chettle House, Dorset
The garden front
Country Life

45. *Francis & William Smith*
Wingerworth Hall, Derbyshire
The entrance hall
Country Life

46. *Francis & William Smith*
Wingerworth Hall, Derbyshire

INTRODUCTION

tecture may consist with the greatest plainess of the structure.'
He indeed favoured a plain type of house, of finely-cut brick,
unadorned except for a simple pilaster portico. Hursley Lodge,
Hampshire, about 1720, is by him, as are his own house at
Warbrooks nearby, 1724, and Iver Grove, Buckinghamshire,
in 1722. Some Hampshire houses incline to a more vigorous
Baroque, notably Herriard Park, about 1700 (47) and Avington
Park, some five years later, with its huge portico and detailed
Baroque entrance door. It was probably a matter of training,
for James was brought up in the School of Greenwich Hospital
and never did quite escape from those influences. Similarly the
houses of Giacomo Leoni are marked by a grandeur of scale
that betrays his training at the Court of the Elector Palatine
in Dusseldorf. As the editor of the first English translation of
Palladio's *Quattro Libri*, he might have possessed all the creden-
tials to perform a neo-Palladian role in competition with Colen
Campbell. But his earlier houses such as Carshalton Park, Surrey, about 1723 (48), or Lyme Park, Cheshire, about 1725 (49)
possess a certain Continental air that sets him firmly in the
Baroque camp. A house such as his Lathom House,

47. *John James*
Herriard Park
Model of the house

48. *Giacomo Leoni*
Carshalton Park, Surrey
Engraving from Leoni's *Alberti*, 1728

49. *Giacomo Leoni*
Lyme Park, Cheshire
Country Life

50. *Giacomo Leoni*
Lathom House, Lancashire
National Monuments Record

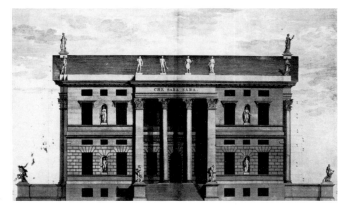

Lancashire, about 1740 (50), built after Gibbs's book was published, marks him as a follower of Gibbs's middle-of-the-road style. Indeed, although neo-Palladianism has been extolled as a national idiom, the provinces outside London never fully accepted Burlington's rigorous style, but took Gibbs's book to heart.

THE NEO-PALLADIAN HOUSE: 1720-1750

John James's letter to the Duke of Buckingham contained implied praise for the work of Inigo Jones, not necessarily prophesying a Jonesian revival, but probably the result of James's experience at rebuilding the north range of Wilton after the fire in 1704. At the time of the letter a house was arising near Wilton that embodied, in its new name, reverence for both Wilton and Amesbury, for the name combined the 'Wil' of one with the 'bury' of the other. Wilbury (19) was 'invented and built' by its owner, William Benson. It can claim to be the first house of the neo-Palladian revival, but its 'invention' was not very great, as the house consisted of the top half of Amesbury laid upon the ground. True invention would have to wait until Colen Campbell and Lord Burlington.

Had it not been for Campbell, Wilbury might have been an isolated incident, and the works of Vanbrugh and Hawks-

moor would have become the models for a national English architecture. When Lord Shaftesbury was advocating a national style in his celebrated *Letter Concerning Design* written in 1712 his tastes were almost certainly for such Baroque works. He nonetheless was aware of a need for a new initative, which would be achieved by Campbell after Shaftesbury's death.

Campbell's arrival upon the scene was as startling as Vanbrugh's at Castle Howard. His first design, dated 1713, for Wanstead House in Essex (51) sounded a death knell for the English Baroque country house. Just how startling Wanstead must have been can be judged by comparing it with Seaton Delaval, still seven years in the future. Wanstead's severe, unrelieved elevations stand out in the pages of volume one of Campbell's *Vitruvius Britannicus*, his eulogy of the work of Jones and declared homage to Palladio. Although *Vitruvius Britannicus* (1715,1717,1725) was at first only intended to display national architecture with Talman, Vanbrugh and Archer to the fore, Campbell organised the Jonesian works—and his own—to demote them by comparison.

Campbell was a thrusting and ambitious man who had no scruples about plagiarising other architects' designs, not the least some prophetic Palladian ones made by his mentor and master, James Smith, in Italy in the 1670s. These Campbell had presumably taken from Smith's portfolios when his student. Ruthlessly, Campbell set out the primary models of the neo-Palladian country house: the Great House, in the guise of Wanstead and Houghton in Norfolk (52), the Villa, with Stourhead

51. *Colen Campbell*
Wanstead House, Essex
Engraved view by George Robertson, 1760s.

52. *Colen Campbell*
Houghton, Norfolk
Engraved by Issac Ware for his *Houghton*, 1735

in Wiltshire (53), and the Villa Rotonda, with Mereworth in Kent (23). It was a heroic achievement whose effect was multiplied because Campbell published these models. In the later works, at Houghton and Mereworth, he began to assemble a grammar for the construction of a neo-Palladian interior, something that he had not been able to do for Wanstead or any house up to about 1720. He took elements from outside and inside Wilton and from exterior elements in Palladio's *Quattro Libri*. His method can be viewed best at Mereworth, in the central hall and adjacent vestibules (24). In his own architecture Campbell never acquired the authority of Burlington or William Kent. When in 1725 the carcase of Houghton was only just up, Kent inexplicably succeeded him as the interior designer of this great house. Unless Campbell had deliberately contracted-out his interior, this must have been unusually galling. By 1722 Burlington had already wrested the commission for building the Westminster Dormitory from William Dickinson, Wren's man. Neo-Palladianism was now firmly under the control of the Architect Earl, although it would not be for long!

It is an oddity in the history of neo-Palladianism that so few of Lord Burlington's works were published. Chiswick Villa and the Westminster Dormitory only appeared—inadequately—in Kent's *Designs of Inigo Jones, with Some Additional Designs* in 1727, but Tottenham Park, Wiltshire, Round Coppice, Buckinghamshire, Northwick Park, Gloucestershire, Petersham Lodge, Surrey and many interior projects, never appeared in print. Had they been published by any of Burlington's acolytes or admirers his influence upon the mainstream of neo-Palladianism would have been so much the greater. Isaac Ware's little book, *Designs of Inigo Jones and Others*, published about 1731, is a case in point. The 53 plates are divided between Jones and Kent, with only one, the gate piers at Chiswick, by Burlington. It is a curious question, and we can only assume that Burlington discouraged publication.

One tragic consequence is that we can only reconstruct Tottenham Park, Wiltshire, begun in 1720, from designs and topographical evidence, although the Burlington house survives within the body of the present early nineteenth-century house by Thomas Cundy. This house was crucial to Burlington's development, as a testing ground for him as an architect. If its

53. *Colen Campbell*
Stourhead
Watercolour of the entrace front by J. Buckler, copied from an earlier view.
National Trust

sources are at this time, like Campbell's, founded in Palladian prototypes, nevertheless they are assembled differently and more intelligently. Tottenham's main claim to distinction rests with its entrance facade (25), the first proper Wilton-inspired front. Tottenham made glaringly clear to Burlington the inadequacies of his own house— by Campbell—in Piccadilly, and within a year Burlington had the materials at hand to become, in Scipio Maffei's words, 'il Palladio e il Jones de' nostri tempi'. These materials were the collection of designs by Palladio, Jones and Webb that Burlington purchased in 1720 and 1721.

Whatever else Chiswick Villa, begun about 1725, has to offer, it will always feature in the annals of architecture as one of the few variations upon the model of Palladio's Villa Rotonda or Capra. Mereworth was the first, and after Chiswick came Nuthall Temple, Nottinghamshire, and Foot's Cray, Kent (54) both of about 1754. The evolution of Chiswick was determined by Burlington's other residences. The family seat and the principal residence of the Boyle family was Londesborough in Yorkshire, a place much frequented by Burlington. Burlington House was the London scene of operations, where Burlington's assistants worked and were lodged. Chiswick was the *villa fructaria et rustica*, the suburban seat in a delicious village near the Thames. It cannot be proven, but it is likely that Burlington intended Chiswick to be an ideal creation, a proper villa to replace the old Jacobean mansion. In 1725 he never intended the old to stand with the new, especially as the new was sited only 50 yards away. When he was forced by personal circumstances in 1733 to use both in tandem his ideal was shattered,

54. *Issac Ware*
Foot's Cray, Kent
Engraving by W. Woollett

and there is circumstantial evidence that his architectural ego was shattered too!

In any context Chiswick would be an exceptional building, but it is unique in Europe for the fanatical manner in which every part is based upon an authority. That authority was to be found in the original designs of Palladio, Jones and Webb, in the paper archaeology of Palladio's fourth book on Roman antiquity, and of Antoine Desgodetz's *Les Edifices antiques de Rome* of 1682, and particularly in Palladio's reconstructional drawings of the Roman Baths. Burlington applied this with such obsession that the fabric of the house became an academic exercise in itself. Burlington was to demonstrate this authority in other works, especially the York Assembly Rooms. He sought to invent or adopt plans that were also founded in antique precedent, hence Chiswick was the first country house to incorporate circular and octagonal rooms with the walls articulated with niches and with screens of columns cutting off semicircular ends of galleries. The plan of Chiswick was perhaps its most potent legacy to the neo-Palladian and Neoclassical country house.

It is surely a criticism of Burlington's method and tuition that none of the young architects gathered into his employ— Henry Flitcroft, Daniel Garrett, or Stephen Wright—sought to recreate this Burlingtonian authority in their own architecture. Either they misunderstood it or they were simply disinclined to take the intellectual trouble. On the whole Burlington had negligible influence upon the form of the country house, though

it may well be that such inventions as his astylar Petersham Lodge, Surrey, about 1733 (55), were simply too clever to be assimilated. Of course, there is that noble exception, Holkham Hall, Norfolk (28) and its architect, William Kent.

Kent had entered Burlington's employ as a painter, graduated to interior decoration, and from about 1729 embraced architecture and landscape gardening. By 1731 he was designing the grand Royal Mews in Charing Cross and his first country house, Kew House in Surrey, for Frederick, Prince of Wales. By 1733 he had begun the enormously influential Gothick Esher Place, Surrey (56), by which time discussions were well under way as to the form of Holkham. If Holkham's origins are to be found in much consulting of portfolios between Burlington and his friend Thomas Coke, the credit for the drawing-board invention must go to Kent, and for the actual construction of the house to Coke's clerk of works, Matthew Brettingham.

The Mews introduced to English architecture what Professor Wittkower aptly described as concatenation. Kent sought a staccato movement in the handling of facades by the advance and

55. *Lord Burlington*
Petersham Lodge, Surrey
From Robert Sayer's engraving

56. *William Kent*
Esher Place, Surrey
Engraving by John Vardy, 1740s

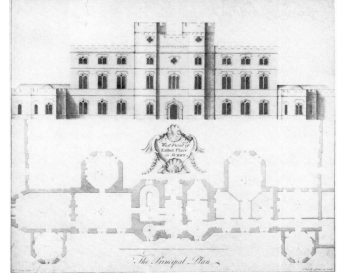

INTRODUCTION

recess of planes, by breaking-up surfaces with rustication or by linking one unit to another with subordinate walls or infills, sometimes topped with balls on concave bases. This hints at the Mannerism of Giulio Romano's Palazzo Del Té, a building Kent certainly studied at first hand. All was brought together at Holkham, where the towers acknowledged Wilton, Houghton and Tottenham; the portico Wanstead, while from Chiswick came the rooms derived from the antique, the Venetian windows set in their relieving arches, and the general grammar of ornament. In this last Holkham was one of the few houses to maintain Chiswick's authority, but significantly that authority is to be found in the paper archaeology of Palladio and Desgodetz, rather than in the original drawings in Burlington's collection. If at Houghton Campbell had advanced the planning of the great house by adapting for his entrance hall the 40ft square cube with surrounding gallery of Jones's Queen's House, Kent's stroke of genius at Holkham was to invent an entirely new hall, of Roman magnificence, of the sort that he might have imagined existing in an Imperial Roman palace. It cleverly combined hall with stairs, bringing the visitor up to the *piano nobile* in one visual progress, for although the stairs were part of the overall spatial design they did not impinge upon the columnar hall itself. This invention cannot be disassociated from what Burlington had achieved at the York Assembly Rooms, with what he called the Egyptian Hall. These columnar episodes at York and Holkham lead on to Robert Adam's hall at Kedleston, in about 1760, and, ultimately, to all those

nineteenth-century Neoclassical and Beaux-Arts museums, stations and hotels all over the world.

We have seen that Campbell had acheived a formula for the systematization of the great house and the villa. Burlington and Kent refined this, and their assistants and contemporaries expanded the villa or reduced the great house, to make many permutations, such as the villa with wings. The architects of this new burst of activity were the neo-Palladians of the second generation, notably Isaac Ware with his Wrotham Park, Middlesex, 1754 (57) and James Paine, the only architect of his generation to comprehend fully and use Kent's concatenated style. Paine achieved mastery in the design of both the small and palatial house (58) as if he had been the natural inheritor of Kent's mantle.

Attempts have been made by historians to find in Burlington and Kent the impetus that establishes neo-Palladianism as a national style. It is perfectly true that Burlington used his influ-

57. Issac Ware
Wrotham Park, Middlesex
From *Vitruvius Britannicus*, IV, 1767

58. James Paine
Stockeld Park, Yorkshire
Country Life

that the prevailing mood was not for didactic authority, and recognized that there was an alternative to Campbell and Burlington, one which appreciated the strength of the tradition that had come down through the great epoch of country house building under William III. Gibbs was able to re-assess all this and to graft on to it his able understanding of Campbell's houses. It was a middle-of-the-road path and the *Book of Architecture* was a powerful instrument. Hence the omnipresent Gibbs style and Gibbs's achievement.

A few architects occupy an uneasy position in the Campbell-Burlington-Kent-Gibbs circle. One such is Roger Morris who starts off as Campbell's assistant, then graduates to become the amanuensis of Lord Pembroke, like Burlington, an Architect Earl. Pembroke seems to have exerted a purifying influence on Morris, and together they broke away from traditional country house models, for example imitating the cubist villa, as at West-combe House, Kent, for Pembroke himself, in 1729 and at Whitton House, Middlesex, about 1732 (35). Nothing as original as these had been seen since Vanbrugh built his small houses, and it cannot be a coincidence that both architects had

59. Burlington & Kent
Houses of Parliament
Design after Kent
Public Record Office

60. Burlington & Kent
Richmond Palace
Model of the building
Victoria and Albert Museum

ence to get jobs for his assistants in the Office of Works, and by so doing enabled Kent to design the Treasury and the Horse Guards. Had fortune smiled more on Burlington and Kent, a new Houses of Parliament might have arisen (59) or a royal palace at Richmond (60), both in a superior Holkham style. Nevertheless it is erroneous to assume that Burlington sought to dictate a national style. He was well aware that that style of compromise with the English Baroque, as epitomised in Gibbs's *Book of Architecture*, was far more popular than his doctrine ever would be.

Gibbs as a country house architect overshadowed all his contemporaries. Between 1714 and 1754 he must have been involved in nearly fifty houses. Few of these can be described as neo-Palladian, but each of them (61) is composed in an architectural language that is sensible and plainly-stated. Gibbs was aware

61. James Gibbs
Plan for a country house, for his *Book of Architecture*
RIBA

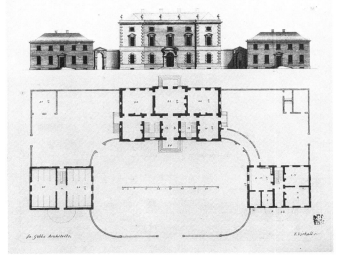

INTRODUCTION

1. *Inigo Jones (1573-1652)*
Design for the façade of a villa
Elevation
Ink and pencil (315 x 465)
See pages 76-77

43. *James Stuart (1713-1788)*
Wimbledon House, Surrey
Design for the decoration and furnishings of a room
Pen, pencil and watercolour (180 x 290)
See pages 160-161

48. *William Newton (1735-1790)*
Highams, Walthamstow, Essex
Preliminary design for Anthony Bacon's house
Plan, and elevation of court front in perspective, with scale
Pencil, pen and wash (335 x 210)
See pages 170-171

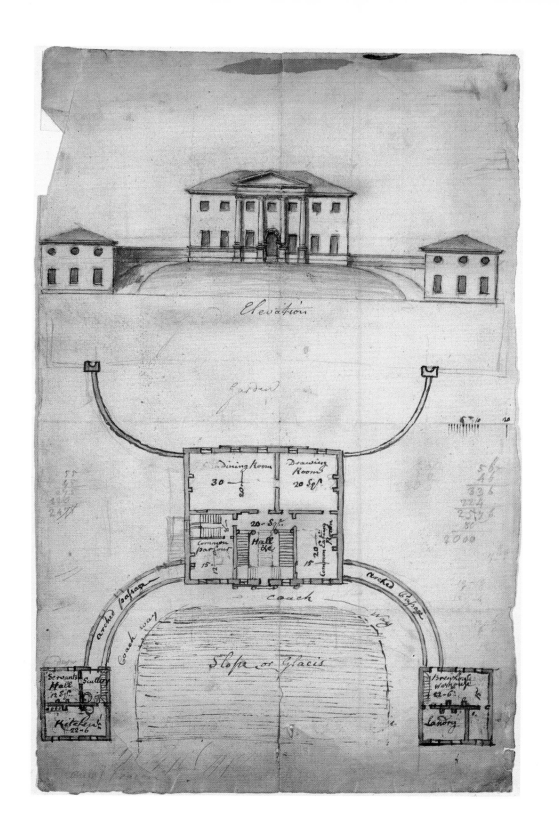

Elevation

Garden

Dining Room
30 —

Drawing Room
20 Sqr

Common Parlour

20 Sqr
Hall

Common Eating Room

Arched passage

Arched Passage

Coach way

Coach

way

Slope or Glacis

Servants Hall

Sculery

Brewhouse Washouse
22-6

Kitchen
22-6

Laundry

31. *William Kent (1686-1748)*
Honingham Hall, Norfolk
Unexecuted design for Gothickising the older house
Elevation with scale
Pen, pencil and wash (330 x 490)

56. *John Buonarotti Papworth (1775-1847)*
Fonthill, Wiltshire
Design for decorating the Boudoir
Plan of ceiling with laid-back wall elevations, with scale
Pen and coloured washes and coloured distemper (330 x 460)
See pages 186-187

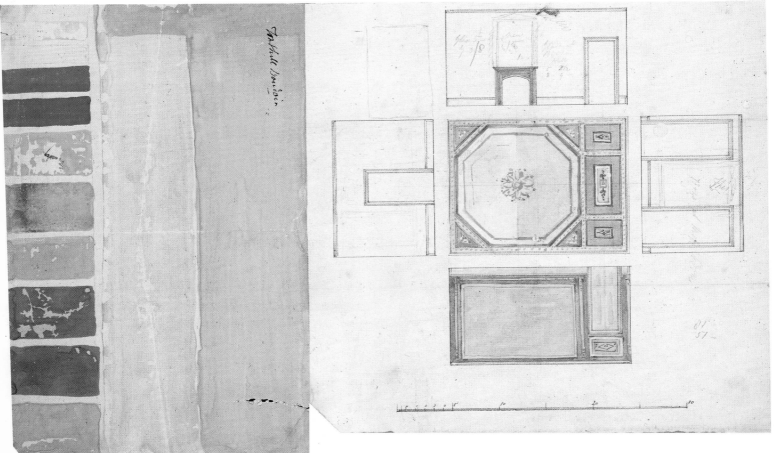

39. Sir William Chambers (1723-1796)
Llanaeron, Cardiganshire
Design for a villa
Elevation of entrance or portico front
Pen and watercolour (365 x 590)
See pages 152-153

FRONT ELEVATION. *Llanaeron*

70. *Augustus Welby Northmore Pugin (1812-1852)*
Scarisbrick Hall, Lancashire
Design for the chimney piece in the Great Hall
Elevation, seen in perspective
Watercolour (320 x 225)
See pages 214-215

68. *Samuel Beazley (1786-1851)*
Bretby Park, Derbyshire
Design for the Countess of Chesterfield's Boudoir
Interior perspective, presented in a simulated frame
Pen and watercolour (410 x 355)

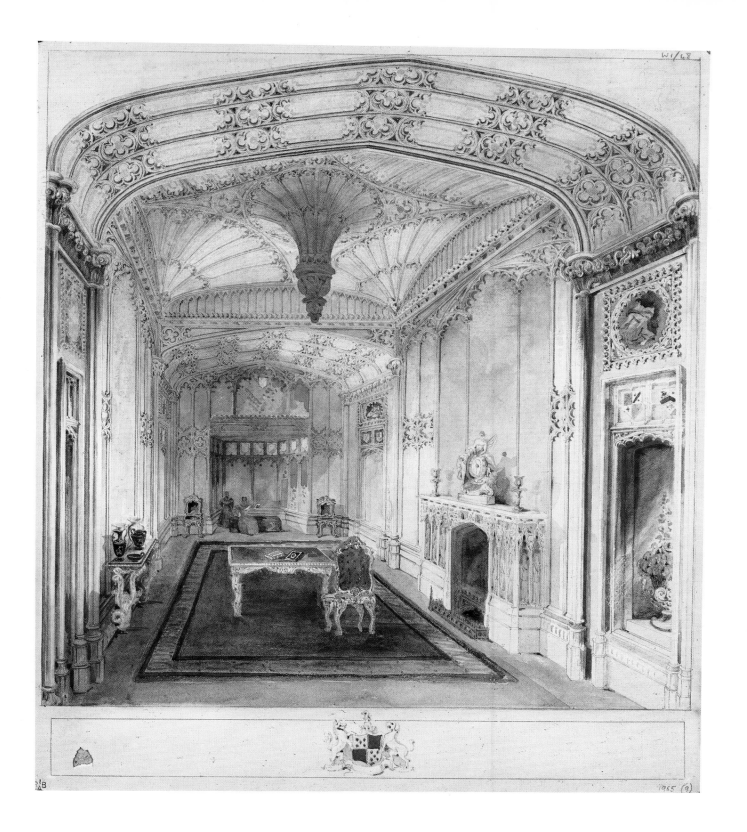

65. Edward Blore (1787-1879)
Goodrich Court, Herefordshire
Perspective
Watercolour (260 x 495)
See pages 204-205

71. Sir Charles Barry (1795-1860)
Highclere Castle, Hampshire
Design for remodelling the old house
Perspective from the north east
Watercolour (495 x 940)
See pages 216-217

worked for the Office of Ordnance. Or there is Isaac Ware, who as the editor of an immaculate edition of Palladio's *Four Books of Architecture* in 1738, dedicated to Lord Burlington, and as editor of the small octavo volume, entitled *Designs of Jones and others*, in 1731 was as close as anyone to Lord Burlington, except for Kent himself. All Ware's buildings, up to Burlington's death in 1752, exercise a discreet Burlingtonian authority, and even a late house such as the noble Amisfield House in Scotland, 1756 (62), possesses a refinement that Gibbs, with the same models, could not achieve. Yet Ware is already bowing to the fashion for the Rococo (63), if the French-styled interiors at Woodcote Park, Surrey, about 1750, are by him (those at Chesterfield House in London, certainly are). But it matters not, for even if they are by John Vardy, as may be possible, here is a dedicated follower of Kent moving away from Burlington's Rule of Taste.

It was Vardy who, at about this time, could offer Lord Milton the choice of a Kentian Gothick or a Classical design for his house at Milton Abbey in Dorset (64). Vardy was partial to Kent's Gothick, for not only did he engrave the designs for Esher, but published many more Gothick designs in *Some Designs of Mr Inigo Jones and Mr William Kent*, 1744, a book that spread the fashion for Georgian Gothick concurrently with Batty Langley's *Ancient Architecture restored*, 1741, the textbook for the Gothick orders.

The spread of what has become known generically as Georgian architecture owes its strength to the phenomenon of the English architectural pattern book and treatise, and if Gibbs's book was the aristocrat of this literature, those by Batty Langley and William Halfpenny were its working-class representatives, advocates of a style diluted from Campbell, Kent and Gibbs and freely borrowing from their engravings. Throughout England there were, and still are, thousands of houses that owe something to Gibbs. They could hardly be called neo-Palladian, and at most might just as well be called Palladian or Georgian. They represent a mean, and a team of builder/architects such as William and Francis Hiorne of Warwick, themselves the successors to the Smiths of that town, produced in their design for Gopsall Hall, Leicestershire in the 1750s (65), the average type of provincial country house. To

62. *Issac Ware*
Amisfield House, East Lothian
National Monuments Record, Scotland

63. *Issac Ware*
Woodcote Park
The chimney-piece
Museum of Fine Arts, Boston

64. *John Vardy*
Milton Abbey, Dorset
Alternative elevations
RIBA

65. *William & Francis Hiorne*
Gopsall Hall, Leicestershire
Design for the house
RIBA

such as Lord Burlington, this average might often have seemed quite foreign. This can be demonstrated at Rushbrooke in Suffolk (66) where a bumpkin sort of provincial builder has made an appealing attempt to modernize an old Jacobean two-storied entrance hall.

Of course there were always those who exercised a quality of architecture somewhere between Chiswick and Gopsall. Two out of dozens of provincial practicioners may be singled out. Matthew Brettingham went on from Holkham to build handsome but plain houses, all affected somewhat by his lessons there. For example, Euston Hall, Suffolk (67) of about 1750 is an essay in the tower-house manner. Another East Anglian architect was John Sanderson whose designs (68), for all their distinction, lack sparkle. Sanderson appears to have been an efficient and well-placed contractor and builder for a number of amateur gentlemen architects; thus he was responsible for several richly-ornamented plasterwork interiors, including Hagley Hall, Worcestershire, in about 1760 (69).

No better contrast with Hagley can be made than with one of Henry Flitcroft's last rooms at Woburn Abbey (70) before he died in 1761. Here (71) is a neo-Palladian chimney-piece of Kent's type combined with a ceiling based upon Robert Wood's *Ruins of Balbec* published in 1757. The re-discovery of these ancient civilisations and cultures was to have a profound effect on design, and provide the materials for generations of Neoclassical architects to construct a new style.

66. Rushbrooke, Suffolk
The Great Hall
National Monuments Record

67. *Matthew Brettingham*
Euston Hall, Suffolk
The garden front
National Monuments Record

68. *John Sanderson*
Design for a house
RIBA

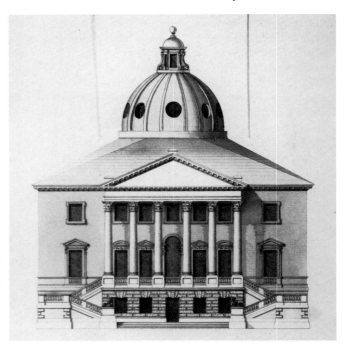

INTRODUCTION

THE NEOCLASSICAL OR GEORGIAN HOUSE: 1750-1800

There is no clear dividing line between neo-Palladian and Neo-classical houses, not the least because Burlington, with his dependence upon antique Roman sources, was in a sense a Neo-classical. No-one recognized this more than Robert Adam did, even if only instinctively. We may seek to identify a fragment of interior decoration as an omen of the new style but we cannot point to one particular country house and say that from this point on all country houses are Neoclassical. If any one type enshrines the new movement it is the villa as it developed in parallel to the great house.

Roger North described the late seventeenth-century house as 'a sort of village or rather city' and the primary seat of a family would remain like this until the 1870s. While the villa emerges as a model in the early years of the eighteenth century only rarely is it an alternative to a primary seat. Its role was that of an addi-tional and usually suburban residence—hence the villas on the Thames outside London from Chiswick to Twickenham. When a villa was required to be the principal residence, as Stourhead in Wiltshire was for a branch of the Hoare family, the compact plan of five bays to the front and perhaps three on the side was no longer sufficient. Stourhead was a villa in front (20) but the plan was broadened to give ambitious 'fronts' on the sides and to provide eight rooms on a floor. There were other incentives to re-assess the needs of a family in terms of architectural language. The older family seats were generally in

69. *John Sanderson*
Hagley Hall, Worcestershire
The white hall
Country Life

70. *Henry Flitcroft*
Woburn Abbey
The garden front
Country Life

71. *Henry Flitcroft*
Woburn Abbey
State bedroom
Country Life

their ancient manorial situations near village and church, if not in close proximity to both. The pressures of changing taste in garden and landscape design brought the house out of the clutches of the village to a place in the park, or else the village and church were removed and the house rebuilt on its old site. Therefore, by about 1730 architects were being challenged to

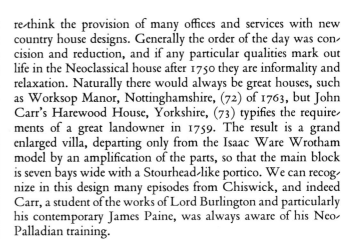

re-think the provision of many offices and services with new country house designs. Generally the order of the day was concision and reduction, and if any particular qualities mark out life in the Neoclassical house after 1750 they are informality and relaxation. Naturally there would always be great houses, such as Worksop Manor, Nottinghamshire, (72) of 1763, but John Carr's Harewood House, Yorkshire, (73) typifies the requirements of a great landowner in 1759. The result is a grand enlarged villa, departing only from the Isaac Ware Wrotham model by an amplification of the parts, so that the main block is seven bays wide with a Stourhead-like portico. We can recognize in this design many episodes from Chiswick, and indeed Carr, a student of the works of Lord Burlington and particularly his contemporary James Paine, was always aware of his Neo-Palladian training.

Under Sir William Chambers, and more so by Sir Robert Taylor, the villa would be refined and sharply chiselled (74). Better than anyone, Taylor could combine so successfully octagonal, square and circular rooms with a spatially complex stair, and if any one external feature marks out the later villa from the earlier one, it is the canted exterior bay reflecting an octagonal room behind. Chambers's villas tended to be refinements of neo-Palladian ones, although at Duddingstone House, Midlothian, 1763 (39b) he achieved an almost perfect temple-form. James Wyatt, who commanded a larger country house practice than any of his contemporaries, not excepting Robert Adam, could offer his client almost any permutation of styles, Classical (75), Gothick and castellated, and it is difficult to begin even to identify a canon in Wyatt's country house designs, so varied are they. Apart from such extraordinary inventions as Robert Adam's Scottish castle or baronial style works, as original as anything since Juvarra and the Piedmontese country house, Neoclassical houses are simply variations on a Classical theme or derivatives in a castellated or Gothick style of Horace Walpole's Strawberry Hill or Kent's Esher Place.

Neoclassicism proper really emerges as a style with the interior. Through the 1740s and early 1750s architectural travellers such as James Stuart became aware of fresh sources of inspiration, in Greece, at Spalatro, and from excavations of ancient Roman buildings in Rome or southern Italy. What

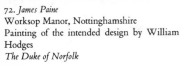

72. James Paine
Worksop Manor, Nottinghamshire
Painting of the intended design by William Hodges
The Duke of Norfolk

73. John Carr
Harewood House, Yorkshire
J. Buckler's view of the south front, 1817

74. Sir Robert Taylor
Harleyford Manor, Buckinghamshire
Painting by Francesco Zuccarelli
The Warde Collection

75. James Wyatt
Henham Hall
Design by Wyatt, 1793
East Suffolk Record Office

INTRODUCTION

marks out a student such as Chambers or Adam in the fifties from a William Kent thirty years earlier, are the bundles of drawings they brought back with them, recording ancient and modern Italy and intended as future models. They returned loaded with ideas, and when they settled in London at the beginning of their careers these drawings formed, as it were, their own encyclopedias. It was natural that the interior rather than the exterior should be a suitable vehicle for the ornamental part of antique decoration, for an interior can contain some innovative detail or element much more easily than an exterior might. Stuart's early Neoclassical interiors for Wimbledon House (42) or Kedleston, around 1757-58, are perhaps the earliest attempts to impose the style upon an English room. Adam, supremely jealous of Stuart, was still learning his antique trade, as can be seen by comparing a Wimbledon design with one by Adam (77) for Shardeloes, Buckinghamshire, in 1761. The gap, however, did not stay great for long, and by the time Chambers had designed his fully Neoclassical ceiling at Buckingham House in 1763 (43) Adam had already mastered, in the same palace (78) what would become no less than the 'Adam style', perhaps the most popular of the Georgian age: certainly the most copied, and, if by a Bonomi, (79) as good as anything

Adam could offer, but otherwise so often weakened and contaminated in the copying. Every room boasted some filigree work in the ceiling or a panel of grotesque decoration on the wall

76. Neoclassical wall decoration
Laid-back plan

77. *Robert Adam*
Shardeloes, Buckinghamshire
Plan
RIBA

78. *Robert Adam*
Buckingham House, London
Ceiling of the japaned bedroom
From Adam, *Works in Architecture*, I, 1773

79. *Joseph Bonomi*
House in Portman Square, London
Interior perspective

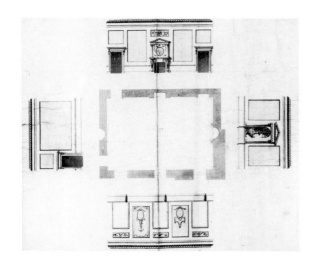

(76), usually made into an ineffective composition. It had been Adam's genius to introduce movement into his interiors and enhance the play of light and shade by the skilful arrangement of decoration, made more potent by his colourings. Chambers tended to be more Roman. His interior decoration was masculine rather than feminine, concentrating perhaps upon the

chimney-piece and the ceiling. Wyatt would play any game, and at his best could be as effective as Adam or Chambers, and sometimes outdo them all.

Long before the Greek Revival became a style that could produce a country house model from identifiable Greek originals, Greek elements had appeared in interiors, notably by James Stuart, decorating a chimney-piece or forming an ornamental frieze. But before the late years of the century no country house could boast a proper Greek-inspired interior. It was different with the importation of the Louis XVI style from France. Chambers had always been a Francophile, for he had been trained in France, not in England, and his interiors at Somerset House in the mid-1770s, are as French as anything in France. From 1783 Henry Holland was designing French interiors at Carlton House for George, Prince of Wales, although many of these, including the staircase (80), reflect Chambers in style. So it can be said that from the eighties onwards the Louis XVI style was not necessarily an alternative style, but its components would be one more reservoir from which architects and decorators could draw. By 1800, although already the more filigree and effeminate extremes were out of fashion, the options were for the Adam style; for the Chambersian Roman manner that Wyatt had magisterially produced at Dodington Park in Gloucestershire, from 1798; obviously for the Neo-Gothic of Wyatt's Lee Priory, 1785, or as demonstrated by William Porden at Eaton Hall, Cheshire, in 1804 (81), and for a mild form of Louis Seize that Holland had elegantly invented for Southill House, Bedfordshire, in 1796. Naturally there were exceptions to the rule, not the least Sir John Soane, whose experiments at the Bank of England would lead to his own idiosyncratic style, one that would be misunderstood and plundered by his contemporaries during the Regency. Soane's Tyringham Hall, Buckinghamshire (52) of 1793 was a villa of distinct Parisian derivation, and Soane's influence was conveyed not so much by first-hand study of his buildings as by his *Plans... of Buildings*, 1788 and *Sketches in Architecture*, 1793. Apart from these mainstreams of style there were the exotics: in the Anglo-Indian style at S.P Cockerell's Sezincote House, Gloucestershire, 1805 (82), Thomas Baldwin's Hafod House, Cardiganshire, built between about 1786 and 1807 (83) or John

80. *Henry Holland*
Carlton House, London
The staircase, from Pyne's *Royal Residences*

81. *William Porden*
Eaton Hall, Cheshire
Design for a parlour
Country Life

82. *C.P. Cockerell*
Sezincote House, Gloucestershire
The garden front

INTRODUCTION

Nash's Indian palace at the Brighton Pavilion, Sussex, 1815, or in the Italian Neoclassical style at Ickworth House, Suffolk, designed in Italy (84) by Mario Asprucci and built by Francis Sandys from 1796. Overall John Nash is perhaps the best yard‑stick of country house style at the turn of the century, for not only was he a master at improvising upon a whole gamut of styles, but he was also the most skilful *pasticheur* of all time, as his excellent design for Rockingham House, Ireland, in 1810 shows (85). Here in one Neoclassical composition he has ele‑gantly encapsulated the best of his Neoclassical forebears.

So far the traditional form of the classical country house has only been modified by variation in elevation or by ornamental attachments: in effect the neo‑Palladian house conflated with Neoclassical ornament. The real move away occured when some architects attempted to invent the neo‑Greek house. There had always been neo‑Greek porticoes, such as George Dance's Doric one at Stratton Park, Hampshire, in 1803; it was quite another matter with a house built nearby at Grange Park just two years later. There William Wilkins attempted—most successfully—to introduce the Greek 'temple beauties' into an English house (51).

At the same time the influence of theories of the Picturesque were loosening the formal restraints of classical plans, so that William Donthorne's Bure Homage, Hampshire, (86) although neo‑Greek outside, is now, in 1835, almost Pic‑turesque in plan. Inside such houses a matching Neo‑Greek style was the exception rather than the rule. This was left to the real exponents of the free classical style in such rogue houses as the Deepdene in Surrey. Most country houses that affected some neo‑Greek taste possessed interiors that can only be des‑cribed as Greco‑Roman. Benjamin Dean Wyatt's interior, for example, for a palace for the Duke of Wellington in 1815 (87) could also serve as the entrance hall of Grange Park. By 1835 J. B. Papworth could offer what he described as a 'Modern Grecian Taste', or what was called Late Regency, a style widely adopted. Papworth provides us with the best measure of the mean in taste between 1820 and 1840.

83. *Thomas Baldwin*
Hafod House, Cardiganshire
The entrance front
National Library of Wales

84. *Mario Asrpucci*
Ickworth, Susex
Model
National Trust

85. *John Nash*
Rockingham House, Ireland
Perspective design
Sir John Summerson

86. *William Donthorne*
Bure Homage, Hampshire
National Monuments Record

87. *Benjamin Dean Wyatt*
Waterloo Palace
Design for the hall
RIBA

88. *Horace Walpole*
Strawberry Hill
Engraving from Walpole's *Description...*, 1784

The Picturesque Country House

Let us discard the several hundred thousand words written by Uvedale Price, Richard Payne Knight, Humphry Repton and William Gilpin on the Picturesque as tedious and boring. It is sufficient to know that the theorists and practitioners of the Picturesque invoked the painter's eye to create out of landscape and buildings a composed picture. As it could be also argued that William Kent very decidedly composed as a painter, or that Capability Brown, in siting his house and arranging his clumps and groves, also viewed his compositions pictorially, some historians have brought the Picturesque back to Sir John Van-brugh. Where does it all begin and where does it end is indeed an open question, especially as many Elizabethan mansions were not only sited in a manner that would have received the approba-tion of Price and Knight, but were eminently picturesque in style. All we can really say is that a Picturesque attitude towards the shape and plan of a house and its situation coalesced as a style around 1800, when architects began to arrange the silhouettes of their houses so that they might appear artlessly contrived. It was this aspect more than any other that produced the asymmetrical plan, and it does perhaps need to be stated that asymmetry of this sort in planning is an English phenemenon.

Strawberry Hill in Middlesex (88) has often been cited as the first asymmetrical house designed as such, but this is not entirely true because the house grew asymmetrically, from about 1750, as a result of whim rather than plan. Nor, pushed up against the public road, can its position truly be called pic-turesque. This was not the case with Payne Knight's Downton

77. *William Burges (1827-1881)*
Knightshayes, Devon
Design for the library
Elevation of chimney wall with half plans of chimney jambs
Pen and wash (445 x 640)
See pages 228-229

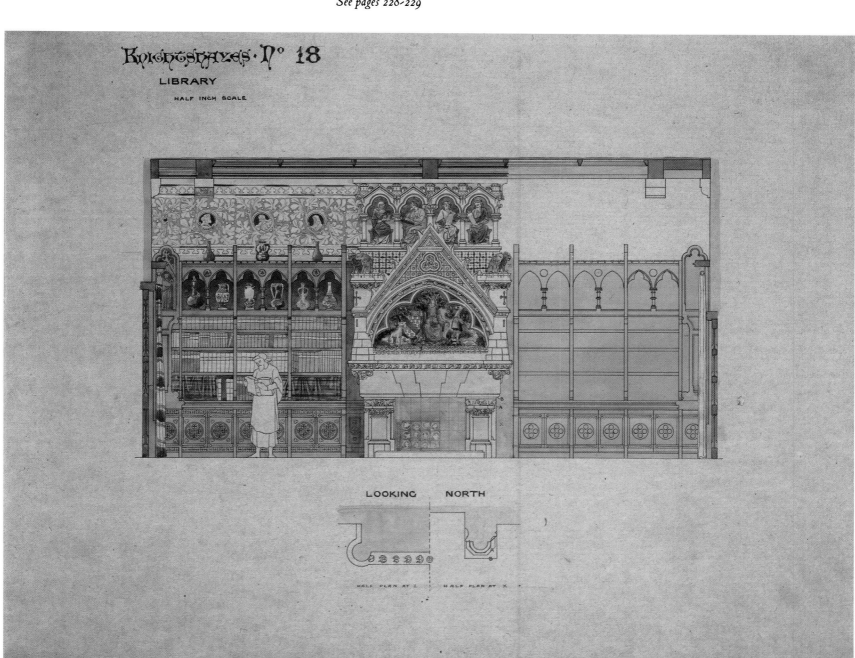

85. *Axel Hermann Haig (1835-1912)*
Design for a half-timbered house in the Old English style
Perspective from the garden
Watercolour (420 x 540)
See pages 244.245

78. *John Hungerford Pollen (1820-1902)*
Blickling Hall, Norfolk
Design for the Library chimney-piece
Perspective elevation *Signed JHP*
Watercolour over pencil and pen (395 x 332)
See pages 230-231

72. *Thomas Allom (1804-1872)*
Highclere Castle, Hampshire
Design for the completion of the entrance hall
Perspective
Pencil and watercolour (980 x 650)
See pages 218-219

89. *Henry Wilson (1864-1934)*
Welbeck Abbey, Nottinghamshire
Design for the Chapel-Library wing
Perspective of the interior of the staircase vestibule
Coloured chalk and watercolour (1155 x 735)
See pages 252-253

88. Sir Ernest George (1839-1922) & Harold Peto (1884-1933)
Poles, Hertfordshire
Design for the Drawing Room
Perspective
Sepia pen and wash (455 x 635)
See pages 250-251

82. Richard Norman Shaw (1831-1912)
Grim's Dyke, Middlesex
Design for a new house
Perspective of back of house from south-east
Pen (495 x 670)
See pages 238-239

90. Sir Reginald Blomfield (1856-1943)
Whittington, Medmenham, Buckinghamshire
Design for new house
Perspective
Watercolour (280 x 560)
See pages 254-255

76. Samuel Sanders Teulon (1812-1873)
Elvetham Hall
Design for new house
Perspective of the garden side
Watercolour
See pages 226-227

93. *Sir Edwin Lutyens (1869-1954)*
Castle Drogo, Devon
Sheet of preliminary perspective studies for exteriors
Pen, pencil and crayon on squared paper (405 x 530)
See pages 260-261

Castle, Herefordshire, an irregular castle built from 1774 on, with an effective massing of towers and outworks. Downton, and James Wyatt's Lee Priory, Kent, about 1785 (89), lead directly to John Nash's own East Cowes Castle, Isle of Wight, built in 1798 (90), and such picturesque castle houses as his Luscombe, Devon, of 1800, Killymoon Castle, Ireland (91), 1809 or Knepp Castle, Sussex, in the same year. At Luscombe we begin to recognize that mixture of Perpendicular Gothic, castellations and crocketted elements that would lead to the creation of the typical early Victorian Mixed Gothic house, of which William Atkinson's Beckett Park, Berkshire, of 1831 (92), is an average example.

89. *James Wyatt*
Lee Priory
From Neal's *Seats*

90. *John Nash*
East Cowes Castle, Isle of Wight
National Monuments Record

91. *John Nash*
Killymoon Castle, Ireland
Perspective view
RIBA

92. *William Atkinson*
Beckett Park, Berkshire
The garden front

93. *James Wyatt*
Norris Castle, Isle of Wight
Drawing by G.S. Repton

94. *James Wyatt*
Cassiobury, Hertfordshire
The entrance front
Lord Essex

95. *Thomas Hope*
The Deepdene, Surrey
Watercolour
RIBA

Nash was a master of what might be described as the free-wheeling plan, synthesising volumetric mass, elevation and setting with convenience. James Wyatt's essays into the castle-style seem tame by comparison, especially judging by his Norris Castle (93), built on the Isle of Wight in 1799. It was William Beckford who began to open Wyatt's eye to the dramatic possibilities of abbey and cathedral as models for a country house. Of course, Fonthill Abbey (57) on its prominence in Wiltshire was so exceptional that it can only be grouped with such rogue houses as the Brighton Pavilion. Because Fonthill was extensively published by John Britton, John Rutter and others, it exerted an influence for its parts out of proportion to its short life, growing from 1796 to 1812 and finally collapsing in 1825. Out of his experiences at Fonthill, Wyatt designed Cassiobury, Hertfordshire, from 1800 (94), a sort of *beau-ideal* of the abbey style transmuted into a country house, and began Ashridge Park, Hertfordshire, (58) in 1808, a vast array of Fonthill details, enlarged after Wyatt's death in 1813 by his nephew Jeffrey Wyatt.

Gothic, with all its irregularities was always seen as the most satisfactory style for a Picturesque house. It was easier to handle than the Classical style, a fact proved by the very few existing examples of Picturesque Classical country houses. Only one such house achieved distinction and fame, of a kind to make it exceptional in all Europe. From 1818 Thomas Hope began to enlarge his fairly average, mid-eighteenth century, Classical house at the Deepdene in Surrey. By 1825 it had been utterly transformed into the ideal Neoclassical house (95) for the age of Romanticism. Hope, his own architect, simply allowed the house to grow by extensions that would push outwards and upwards with towers, screens, galleries, all luxuriously embellished and ornamented with conservatories and flower-decked vestibules. Inside a columnar hall was filled with sculpture, like the museum atrium of today. Deepdene not only recalled Hope's travels in Greece and Asia Minor, but was witness also to his deep reflections on the architecture and decoration of all ages. His architectural achievements are a fascinating parallel to Beckford's, for even before the collapse of Fonthill the 'Caliph' had commissioned the young H. E. Goodridge in 1823 to provide him with an irregular classical house (61) that would not have

INTRODUCTION

been out of place as an extension of the Deepdene; in the result, the style of Beckford's Lansdown Tower in Bath is a free Classical one that delves back as far as the English baroque of Vanbrugh. It would soon become debased, the source of the 'Grecian and Italian' style of the thousands of early Victorian villas that were built on the edge of towns. It contributed to Sir Charles Barry's 'Palazzo Italianate' style, and received the royal Imprimatur when used by Thomas Cubitt for Queen Victoria at Osborne House, Isle of Wight, in 1843 (96).

If by 1843 dilemmas of style were already apparent in England, they were not so evident in Scotland for there Robert Adam's version of Scottish Baronial was grafted onto a living tradition. Then Robert Lugar transported Nash's Picturesque, castle manner from the south to Tullichewan Castle, Dumbartonshire in 1808 (60), although his designs always looked better in aquatint in his books than in reality. Both William Burn and later David Bryce would build upon the Nash legacy. In England the recipe served as Mixed Gothic produced hundreds of mediocre, irregular houses. In the hands of J.A. or G.S. Repton the style might have distinction and in his Tudoresque gabled style the young Anthony Salvin advertised, in houses like Mamhead, Devonshire, (97) 1827, and later at his perfect Scotney Castle, Kent, the arrival of a new luminary upon the scene who would revolutionise the building of castles.

Castle building became serious just as A.W.N. Pugin was invoking a new authority in the design of a country house, at Scarisbrick, Lancashire, in 1838. There would always be rogue castles of little immediate influence, notably Penrhyn Castle, Caernarvonshire, of 1825 by Thomas Hopper. One of the most powerful expressions of the revived Romanesque style in England, his design draws upon the great twelfth-century castle keeps of Rochester or Castle Hedingham, and the nearby Welsh castles of Harlech and Conwy. It is a pity that Samuel Rush Meyrick selected Blore rather than Hopper when building his Goodrich Court, Herefordshire, in 1828 (98). One suspects that Blore's superb ability as a watercolourist seduced many of his clients; only upon close scrutiny do his appealing renderings show their lack of any feeling for volumes. There is a world of difference between a design such as Goodrich and a castle invention by Salvin, as his studies for Peckforton Castle,

96. *Thomas Cubitt*
Osborne House, Isle of Wight
Design for the house
H.M. Colvin

97. *Anthony Salvin*
Mamhead, Devonshire
Perspective
RIBA

98. *Edmund Blore*
Goodrich Court, Herefordshire
The garden front
National Monuments Record

99. *Alfred Waterhouse*
Eaton Hall, Cheshire
West front
National Monuments Record

100. *William Burn*
Fonthill Abbey, Wiltshire
Sketchbook design
RIBA

101. *C.H. Howell*
St Leonards Hill, Berkshire
The garden front
National Monuments Record
(facing page bottom left)

Cheshire, 1844, (66) demonstrate. Salvin possessed a natural feeling for military architecture, and brought up as he was in the Nash Picturesque tradition he recognized the freedom that the Mediaeval curtain wall gave him in planning. Within that wall he could provide internal comfort and convenience, while uninhibitedly maximising the external effect. Nevertheless almost as soon as Peckforton was finished it was already old-fashioned: Sir George Gilbert Scott thought it the 'height of masquerading'. To a Sir Edwin Lutyens with Castle Drogo,

Devon, in 1909, (93) and Philip Tilden with Hengistbury Head, Hampshire, (94) in 1919, it had all become a great game.

THE VICTORIAN AND EDWARDIAN HOUSE

If we examine Tullichewan or Scotney or any of the houses of the late Picturesque up to about 1830 we would find it difficult to determine from the division of the roofs and the general bulk the whereabouts, for example, of the Great Hall or the kitchen. The external form had been arranged in order to create a particular effect in the landscape, not to represent the functional aspects of the house. The advent of A.W.N. Pugin upon the country house scene changed all this, through his introduction of morality into architecture. For Pugin, every part must be authentic and represent its proper function: the high roof above denoted a Hall, the tall octagonal or pyramidal roof a kitchen. So it is at Scarisbrick Hall, Lancashire, 1836, (70) where Pugin's fanaticism for correct detail introduced into the early Victorian house the sort of pedantry that had made Chiswick less visually pleasing than Mereworth. Other architects rarely exercised this option with such an obsession. But a High Victorian counterpart to Scarisbrick might be Alfred Waterhouse's Eaton Hall, Cheshire, (99) remodelled for the Duke of Westminster from 1870 and the *beau-ideal* of a Ducal house.

Most other Victorian architects of Pugin's generation were receptive to various styles, quite happy to offer their clients Elizabethan, Anglo-Italian, Palladian or Palazzo, the four styles that appealed to Sir Charles Barry. Nothing could be more different from Scarisbrick than Barry's Anglo-Italian Highclere Castle, Hampshire (70) with its Wren-style church, yet they are of the same date, as is William Burn's Stoke Rochford Hall, Lincolnshire (72) in a symmetrical Jacobean style. Burn was one of the most versatile architects of the first half of the century, able to turn out practical and convenient houses in almost any style. His was the remarkable Fonthill Abbey, Wiltshire (100) designed in Scotch Baronial in 1846 for the Marquess of Westminster, but not built—and then to revised designs—until 1856. Generally, Victorian houses of the 1840s on are not adventurous, any more than were those architects who followed Pugin's lead. P.C. Hardwick's Addington Manor, Buckinghamshire of

INTRODUCTION

1856 has a little more vigour than usual, its spiky Gothic with French episodes already dengerating in quality in comparison with Pugin. Or there is Waterhouse's Yattendon Court, 1878, (74) that, with its hard red brick and terracotta detail, might just as well be on the outskirts of Manchester, rather than in rural Berkshire.

Addington reminds us that the Victorians loved the high-roofed French style of Mediaeval romance, and it is often the roof-scapes of Victorian houses that stay in the memory. Thus many architects offered the French chateaux style, whether it be French Gothic or French Louis XIII or Louis XIV, as did C.H. Howell at St Leonard's Hill, Berkshire, (101) a remodelling of a Georgian house in 1875 for a rich copper magnate. The style could hardly have been more appropriate for Nouveau-Riche clients such as the Rothschilds of Wad-desdon Manor, Buckinghamshire, (103) begun in 1841 by G. H. Destailleur and perhaps what we best remember of this sort of French chateaux style in England.

Any account of the Victorian country house must mention the astonishing exceptions to the rule—or the fact that the majority of country houses are of indifferent design. It was not so in the eighteenth century, when architects had to concentrate their minds upon one Classical style or the narrow parameters of the Gothick. In the nineteenth century there would always be such waywards as Teulon or Burges. Not since Pugin had there appeared an architect like William Burges capable of drawing from both Christian and secular sources in Europe as well as the Middle East and of distilling all this into his fan-tastic designs, loading his chimney-pieces, for example, with a rich encyclopaedic array of ornament (102). His Castell Coch in Glamorganshire, designed in 1872 and only halted when Burges died in 1881, gave Lord Bute a Mediaeval fortress (105)

102. *William Burges*
Chimney-piece at Castell Coch
Country Life

103. *C.H. Destailleur*
Waddesdon Manor, Berkshire
Country Life

104. *Henry Clutton*
Minley Manor, Hampshire
RIBA

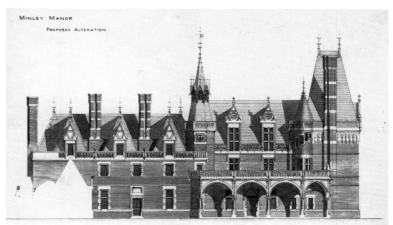

105. *William Burges*
Castell Coch, Glamorganshire
The entrance front
Country Life

106. *Robert Kerr*
Bear Wood, Berkshire
Country Life

107. *E.W. Pugin*
Carlton Towers, Yorkshire
Engraving of Pugin's design
Country Life

that would have made Viollet-le-Duc envious. The only other architect in the nineteenth century that even remotely approached the fantasy of Burges's eclecticism was John Hungerford Pollen, that extraordinary Celt responsible for the strange decorations (77) at Blickling Hall, Norfolk, in 1859.

Another memorable aspect of the Victorian house is its aggressiveness, a quality that seems to accord well with the buccaneering aspect of the Victorian age, as if the new rich demanded vigorous, ugly houses rather than effete and polite ones. This sort of aggression is found in S.S. Teulon's Elvetham Hall, Hampshire, 1859, (75) where the polychromatic and textural effect is carried as high as the roofs with their jazzy patterns in the tiles. A neighbour of Elvetham's is Henry Clutton's Minley Manor of 1858 (104), and its French Gothic seems deliberately anarchic; or there is Robert Kerr's hideous and ponderous Bear Wood, Berkshire (106) 1865, as ungracious as any house of its style could be. This tendency to the ugly has been called the 'Muscular' style, an architectural response to the cult of Victorian manliness. The same response can be seen in a different way, which develops from Scarisbrick Hall, at Carlton Towers, Yorkshire, built by Edward Welby Pugin in 1873 for the swashbuckling Lord Beaumont, to an astonishing design (107) which vigorously married French Late Gothic

to Low Countries Flemish and the French Bastille or Vincennes style. Another line of development can be seen, if we study Shadwell, Norfolk, 1856, a Teulon house with aggressive qualities, where we notice that it adapts into its external fabric the local East Anglian vernacular style of cut stone and flintwork. Teulon used this to produce polychromatic and hybrid effects, but was not unaware that his recognition of the local vernacular and an interest in materials for their own sake was something very much in the air and was to lead to what was called the Old English style.

In one sense there had been an Old English style since the early nineteenth century. As recently as 1848 the fourth and last part of C.J. Richardson's *Studies of old English mansions* had appeared, a work that provided the architect with a whole new range of sources from Elizabethan and Jacobean architecture. W.E. Nesfield has been credited with the invention of the stylistic term 'Old English style' in the context of his studies of old cottages in Warwickshire. Together with Norman Shaw's work, this was to revolutionise the character of British architecture, away from the continental sources of so much High Victorian and towards a genuine interpretation of English vernacular. The real inventor of the style is George Devey, but his reclusive nature, his refusal to exhibit his designs or to allow their publication prevent any assessment of what Nesfield or Shaw knew of his work. In the early 1850s he was designing cottages in a Kent vernacular style at Penshurst, and his training

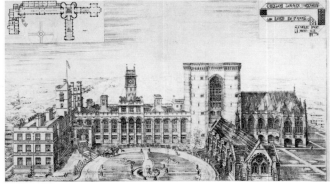

as a watercolourist under J.D. Harding and John Sell Cotman contributed to his appreciation of old cottages and timber-framed houses. Betteshanger, Kent, 1856 (108), is astonishingly prophetic of what Nesfield and Shaw would be doing fifteen years later. What differentiates Nesfield's work, for example at Babbacombe Cliff, Devon, 1876, from Devey, is Nesfield's greater authority over the relationship of plan to elevation. So often, Devey drew enchanting watercolour designs that time and again failed in execution, and this must certainly be said of Betteshanger or of Machareoch House, Kintyre of 1871 (79).

Shaw's Leyswood, Sussex (109) and Grims Dyke, Middlesex, (80) are the best examples of his Old English style. Both were designed in 1870, and both were made the focus of a special type of setting that might be called arboreal. Leyswood had the advantage of a craggy outcrop on the site, to which Shaw made the house respond. It was even then called 'quaint', but Shaw's genius at planning created a convenient house—as if comfort must have priority. Of course, there is not a little in this of Nash's Picturesque sense of composition. Leyswood departs from the traditional park-like setting for the greater country house, not inappropriately for what would become suburban Sussex. As a house in a forest it can be compared to Beauvale Lodge, Nottinghamshire, in 1871 (82) by that other Old English stylist, E.W. Godwin.

The inspiration that Nesfield and Shaw found from their observation of local vernacular building, reappeared only a few miles away from Leyswood at Standen, also in Sussex, but by Philip Webb. The effect is different, being what one might call the manorial farmhouse style, for Webb deliberately exercised restraint. He would not have approved of the dominance that Shaw had given to Leyswood on its crag, or to Cragside, Northumberland, 1870.

In 1872 Webb built Rounton Grange, Yorkshire (110), in a style that shows him looking at English Baroque, but curiously mixed with quasi-Mediaeval detail. His Smeaton Manor, Yorkshire, 1877, has elements of Queen Anne and Georgian. These two houses mark a period that saw the emergence of the Queen Anne style, later called Renaissance. Nesfield had already charted its course with his huge Kinmel in Denbighshire (111) begun in 1868, which at first glance appeared to be in a French

chateau style with its high roofs, but in fact contained much more of Hampton Court. Kinmel is at the beginning of a period wherein Sir Reginald Blomfield's ably-handled Whittington, Buckinghamshire, 1897, stands mid-way in the revival of the

108. *George Devey*
Betteshanger, Kent
The garden front
RIBA

109. *Norman Shaw*
Leyswood, Sussex
National Monuments Record

classical country house. By 1908 Blomfield was demonstrating the Hampton Court manner, laced with Baroque, with houses such as Moundsmere, Hampshire (112), and by 1890 Shaw had gone completely classical at Bryanston, Dorset, and his Chesters, Northumberland, 1891 (113), was an early example of neo-Georgian Baroque, the style that Shaw would soon be demonstrating at the Piccadilly Hotel, Regent Street, 1905.

In the relationship of ground to building, much at Leyswood would have received the approbation of Humphry Repton. This is not to say that either Shaw or Nesfield understood the theories of the Picturesque, but they operated as if they had. After all, the term 'Old English' could be applied to many of Repton's restorations of great Tudor and Elizabethan houses. It is as if the Picturesque had arisen in the late eighteenth century, bobbed up again in the mid-nineteenth, definitely to re-emerge under Sir Ernest George and Sir Edwin Lutyens. George was a most successful contemporary of Nesfield and Shaw, and his large Buchan Hill, Sussex of 1882 (86) is a Picturesque house directly in the tradition of Salvin and Burn, in fact a modern version of Stoke Rochford. At the beginning of the twentieth century Lutyens's Ashby St Ledgers (91) displayed what that master of the Picturesque had learnt whilst in George's office, and pays homage, even if unconsciously, to the north elevation of Salvin's

Harlaxton. It is also Salvin that Lutyens surely honours with the first designs for Castle Drogo, Devon, in 1910. He must have observed that Salvin too liked to play the great game as a castle builder. Only Philip Tilden could have played a greater one if Gordon Selfridge had matched his ambitions at Hengistbury Head (94) with a large enough purse. Hengistbury was not in the Old English style, but its architect was one of the most sensitive restorers of old houses and possessed a sense of the Picturesque combined with an ability to instil drama into his buildings. There is surely a direct line of Picturesque development from Sir John Vanbrugh to Philip Tilden.

When Nesfield was asked to design a small entrance lodge at Kinmel in 1868 just before beginning the great house, he produced a richly-ornamented facade with carved sunflowers and lilies and Japonaiserie roundels. Sunflowers also could be found in the wrought-iron balconies. Similar craft work can be detected in many of Shaw's buildings, not the least on timber-framed gable-ends, and already by the 1860s the chimney-piece was departing from the usual traditional, superimposed model. The interiors of Godwin's Beauvale, 1871, illustrate this perfectly, where the fireplaces may be of cut brick laid in patterns and combined with tile-work and fancy ironwork. Webb's Clouds 1876–1881, described as the 'house of the age' was full of this, as well as being a memorable example of a white-painted interior. Webb had been a partner in the firm dominated by William Morris and founded in 1861, one of the first decorating firms in the modern sense. They would design stained glass, tapestries, wallpapers and tiles, with a concern for the art of craftsmanship in all materials, and applying the same attention to furniture and moveables. This unity of all the arts was what the Arts and Crafts Movement was all about. The same delight in craft-work can be observed in Sir Ernest George's manorial and Elizabethan-style houses or in such evocations of Jacobean rooms as his Poles in Hertfordshire as late as 1890 (87). Poles shows the influence upon the Victorian interior of the antique dealer, for it includes original seventeenth-century pieces, while there are arrangements of porcelain on the cabinets. The interiors at Poles can be usefully compared to the Music Room at Balcombe Place, Sussex, designed in 1899 by Gerald Callcott Horsley, a perfect Arts and Crafts ensemble by one of the

founder members—if not the originator—of the Art Workers' Guild in 1884.

It is obvious that the Arts and Crafts style was not easily assimilated by the greater country house. In fact, Arts and Crafts would become more and more suburban, its tenets being applied more to town houses. It suited the idea of the house in the country rather than the country house, and it is surely relevant that C.F.A. Voysey never designed a proper great country house. Arts and Crafts in the greater houses tends to be episodic: a room here, a smaller wing there, as at Welbeck Abbey in Nottinghamshire, where the chapel and library wing had been begun by J.D. Sedding, and continued after his premature death in 1891 by his faithful disciple Henry Wilson, with a crafted interior (88) that combines metalwork, carved wood, plaster work, stained glass and ornamental tiles. And yet the room has a cosiness that accords ill with the idea of a room in a great country house.

It was an extraordinary act of faith—or folly—to contemplate building a Castle Drogo from 1910 through the First War or Hengistbury Head after the massacres of the War. For by 1900 great country houses were being abandoned, many as a result of the agricultural depression that spread like a disease throughout Britain from 1873. Those years before the First World War were an Indian summer, and few realized that within eight years country houses would come tumbling down. No less than about thirty great houses were demolished in 1920, until in 1970 the total had reached well over 2200. In the black year of 1955 it is reckoned that two and a half houses were demolished every day. Of course, we know that country houses continued to be built, rebuilt or substantially enlarged after 1920 and after 1945, but what is interesting about the period since the First World War is that no longer can we say that this style or that is characteristic. The output was simply too small, and whereas the 'house in the country' flourished on the west coast of America due to the huge demand for such houses, in Britian large new houses are isolated examples. The tradition for building great country houses can be said to have died with Sir Reginald Blomfield in 1943.

The publishers thank the following for permission to reproduce illustrations in the catalogue:
Ashmolean Museum, Oxford 5a; Buckinghamshire County Museum 18b; Courtauld Institute 3b, 25b, 92a; Country Life 3a, 6b, 7b, 9b, 10b, 12a, b, 14a, 16a, b, 17b, 18a, 28a, 34b,c, 39b, 47b, 60b, 67b, 71a,b, 75a, 91a, 93a; Godfrey New Photographs Ltd 15b; A. F. Kersting 30b, 89a; National Monuments Record, 24a, 51b, 61b, 74a,b, 88a; National Monuments Record, Scotland 10a, 34a, 57a, 61c, 89b; R.I.B.A. 4b, 17a, 22c, 23a, 27a,b, 28b, 36b, 50b, 51a,b, 52a, 64a, 69a, 70b, 73a, 85b, 94c; Society of Antiquaries 79a; the Victoria & Albert Museum 7a; the Yale Center for British Art 5b, 80a.

Catalogue of drawings

The works selected for the exhibition are reproduced in the following pages. The main illustration is on the right hand page, with its caption, the descriptive text and supplementary illustrations (numbered *a*, *b*, *c* etc) on the left hand page. A list of the architects and houses discussed will be found on page 264.

Although this design (*1*) has been published as for the Queen's House and therefore dated to 1616, it may well be for a lodge rather than a palace, or at least not for a palace in the peculiar situation of the present Queen's House set across the public road. It matters not, simply that here is an extraordinarily prophetic design anticipating the neo-Palladian villa of the early eighteenth century.

Lord Burlington, who had bought the collection of designs by Palladio, had by 1721 discovered in the portfolios the design for this exhibited villa that must have immediately taken his attention as conforming to a neo-Palladian ideal. Here, then, was confirmation in the hands of the great master. Unfortunately Burlington, unable to distinguish between the draughtsmanship of Palladio and Jones did not recognize that this ideal design was by the latter, having found its way, as did many other designs by Jones, into Palladio's portfolios by mistake. Burlington had Henry Flitcroft redraw it (*1a*), but in so doing misinterpreted Jones's incomplete elevation. It had been Jones's intention to express the three bays of the first floor under the pediment as a loggia *in antis*. But it has been transposed into a pilaster portico, uncommonly like that designed in 1723 by Campbell for Lord Herbert at Pembroke House, Whitehall.

1a

THE STUART HOUSE

1. Inigo Jones (1573-1652)
Design for the façade of a villa
Elevation
Ink and pencil (315 x 465)
Lit. and repr. Margaret Whinney, 'An Unknown Design for
a Villa by Inigo Jones', *The Country Seat, Studies In The History
of the British Country House* (ed. Howard Colvin & John Harris), 1970, pp 33-5; John Harris, *The Palladians*, 1981, pl 3
RIBA DRAWINGS COLLECTION

THE STUART HOUSE

2a

Jones may well qualify as a master designer of chimney-pieces, an element of interiors that for obvious reasons is essentially north European in context; there were in 1623 few engraved models. For St James's Palace Jones used the *nappa* or chimney opening from Scamozzi (his only chimney offering), and he was already improvising upon the design of the overmantel. When Jones was ordered to complete the unfinished Queen's House at Greenwich in 1630 his vocabulary for interior decoration was already becoming enriched by more eclectic sources. This design for a chimney-piece (*2a*) is one of Jones's greatest acts of draughtsmanship, elevating him to the pantheon of European draughtsmen. The broken-pedimented chimney surround is adapted from Jean Barbet's *Livre d'Architecture, d'Autels, et de Cheminées* of 1633; the drawings of *putti* demonstrate his love for Parmigianino and the Carracci. By 1636 at Oatlands (*2*), a Tudor palace formerly one of Queen Anne of Denmark's favoured country retreats that had been granted to Queen Henrietta Maria in 1627, Jones was aware of other engraved sources, notably Barbet. However, Jones was never a slavish copyist, but transmuted an idea into something peculiarly Jonesian. The Oatlands drawing is a wonderfully fluid study, a vigorous demonstration of Jones's mastery as a draughtsman.

Henry VIII's palace was demolished in the 1650s. It became the seat and park of Lord Lincoln in the eighteenth century and although Lord Lincoln's park remains, today the site of the Tudor palace is covered by a housing estate.

2. Inigo Jones (1573-1652)
Oatlands Palace, Surrey.
Elevation
Insc. (by Jones) *first scizzo chimney peece for Oat-lands 1636*
Pen and pencil (260 x 190)
Lit. The History of The King's Works (ed. H.M. Colvin), IV (1485-1660), Part II, 1982, 216-17
RIBA Drawings Collection

The Queen was Henrietta Maria, who in 1626 ordered a sequence of alterations that included a major new chapel and redecorations of many of the older rooms in this great town palace, originally built by the Protector Somerset, between 1548 and 1551. None of Inigo Jones's decoration survives in its original state, but the accounts for the 'New' Closet provide a vivid picture of the richness and colour that would be found in one of these royal apartments. The architrave, frieze and cornice of the doorcase were carved by Zachary Taylor, painted like white marble and enriched in gold. Around the room were panels each filled with grotesques (in probably red, blue, yellow and gold) whilst the framework was gilded and had flowers painted at each intersection. The inner face of the stone window had gold arabesques on white and a band of gold next to the glass, and all the metal and ironwork was gilded. The chimney-piece was white and gilt below and blue and gilt above. The ceiling was white with a shadowed and gilded foliage in the centre.

Inigo Jones's 'Scizo of the Great Doure in the Banqueting House', dated 1619, his earliest surviving design for any interior element (3a) reflects an interest in contemporary Mannerism, in memory perhaps of Scamozzi's doors in the Collegia anteroom of the Doge's Palace in Venice. There is evidence here, at the beginning of Jones's career as a professional architect, of a robustness that would give way to more elegance and femininity.

Jones's design for an exterior window or *aedicule* at the royal chapel at Somerset House (3b) is dated 1632 and in the manner of Carlo Fontana. By the 1630s Jones was responsive to many more sources not only in Rome and Florence but in France, bearing in mind that the Queen was French.

3. *Inigo Jones (1573-1652)*
Somerset House, London
Design for the doorcase in the Queen's New Cabinet Room
Elevation with faint outline of section of jambs
Pencil and pen (320 x 360)
Lit. & reprd. Inigo Jones and John Webb (RIBA Catalogue), ed. John Harris; *The History of the King's Works*, ed. H. M. Colvin, IV, 1982, 262ff
RIBA DRAWINGS COLLECTION

4b

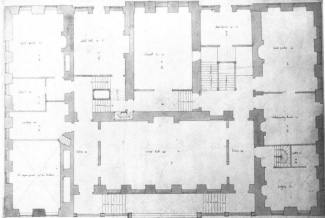

4a

Raynham Hall was begun by its owner Sir Roger Townsend in 1619, with the aid of mason called William Edge, who appears to have been the executive of Sir Roger's ideas. The house was built very slowly (Sir Roger living in the old house nearby) and work on it may have stopped and started with substantial alterations. For example, when the walls were rising Sir Roger and Edge made visits to London and the Netherlands.

In the absence of any surviving country house designed by Inigo Jones, Raynham is a precious reminder of what a house by Jones might have looked like, for it can be described as Jonesian and nothing less. Indeed, Sir Roger must either have consulted Jones or seen Jones's drawings at Newmarket Palace, a stop on the road from Raynham to London. There are many allusions and references to Jones's drawings made from about 1616 to about 1620, as well as to the actual designs for the Prince's Lodging at Newmarket. Raynham's gabled wings are reminiscent of a design by Jones for Sir Fulke Grevile's house in Holborn and its noble Ionic portico is a country cousin of the Scamozzian Newmarket design.

There is some evidence that the spaces between the gabled wings and the centre-piece were filled-in after 1660. (4b) shows Raynham Hall viewed from the south-east and as altered after 1670.) If this was really the case, Raynham's portico would have been a proper temple-feature, burrowing back into the body of the house and would thus have been reminiscent of Palladio's Villa Maser. Palladian influences can also be seen in the ground floor plan of Raynham Hall (4a) with its strong echoes of the woodcut of Palladio's Villa Poiana.

THE STUART HOUSE

4. I.E. (possibly a member of the Edge family)
Raynham Hall, Norfolk
Survey elevation of the east front
Pen, pencil and wash (420 x 580)
Lit. & reprd. John Harris, 'Inigo Jones And The Prince's Lodging at Newmarket', *Architectural History*, vol. 2, 1959, pp 26–40
RIBA Drawings Collection

5a

Jones's work at Wimbledon Palace is imprecisely documented. King Charles purchased the palace for Queen Henrietta Maria in 1639. By July 1641 Nicholas Stone was supplying new chimney-pieces and the Declared Accounts show payments made to Jones *for building and repairing at our house at Wimbledon.* At the same time André Mollet was laying out the gardens. What Jones effected was the addition of a large wing to the west side of this Jacobean house. The pencilled drawing for the entablature (5) would suggest a major element of a wall of a room where the centre breaks forward. Between the mod-illions are inset or painted classical reliefs; indeed, as Jones's inscription states, they were part painted and part in relief. Other designs by Jones include one (5a) for a frieze, possibly for part of a decoration commissioned by Queen Henrietta Maria, which could have been in plaster relief, and another (5b), with Queen Henrietta Maria's initials, for a vertical panel of decoration in the painted style of John de Critz or Matthew Gooderick.

5b

THE STUART HOUSE

5. *Inigo Jones (1573-1652)*
Wimbledon Palace, Surrey
Design for the decoration of a frieze of an entablature
Detail of part of entablature, cornice and the frieze decoration
Insc. (by Jones) *for freeses at Winbelton/part of Relieve parte painted*
Pen and pencil (155 x 270)
RIBA Drawings Collection

THE STUART HOUSE

6b

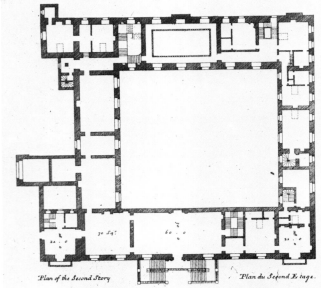

'Plan of the Second Story   'Plan du Second Étage.

6a

The south front of Wilton as it stands today with its terminating towers or pavilions has been celebrated for over 250 years as a venerated work by the great master Inigo Jones. In fact, Jones's connection with Wilton is tenuous. He certainly made some designs for interiors either destroyed or never executed, but he did not design the famous south front as it was built. In 1636 Philip, 4th Earl of Pembroke, contracted with Isaac de Caus to demolish the front of the old Tudor house and to build the new 'according to the Platt which is agreed'. No-one would deny that de Caus's design is a noble thing, but it does not survive the test of comparison with Jones's documented designs. It is what might be expected of de Caus, who was a great garden designer and grotto-maker, a hydraulics expert, learned in music and harmonics, a French Huguenot with decided Gallic tastes, but not a great architect. Like Nicholas Stone he was of subordinate quality in the First Stuart Court. Two years after the fire in 1647, rehabilitation works were carried out under the supervision of John Webb, perhaps with, as John Aubrey commented years later, 'the advice and approbation of Mr. Jones'. It was then that the pavilion towers were built and the hipped roof replaced by a flat one with a balustrade, giving the front its time-honoured form and making it the admired model for the neo-Palladian tower house. For by 1700 Wilton had entered into the Inigo Jones mythology, and the contributions of Isaac de Caus and John Webb had been forgotten. The plan of Wilton engraved for Campbell's *Vitruvius Britannicus*, 1715, (6a) is as after the fire of 1647; the south front is to the bottom. The north range may be by John James, and built after the fire in 1704. It has still not been determined if the towers on the north front are of Webb's period, or subsequent to the fire (6b shows Wilton today, seen from the south-east).

6. Isaac de Caus (died c. 1656)
Wilton House, Wiltshire
Design for the south front
Elevation
Pen and some pencil (155 x 445)
Lit. & reprd. H.M. Colvin, 'The South Front of Wilton
House', *Archaeological Journal*, CXI, 1955
RIBA DRAWINGS COLLECTION

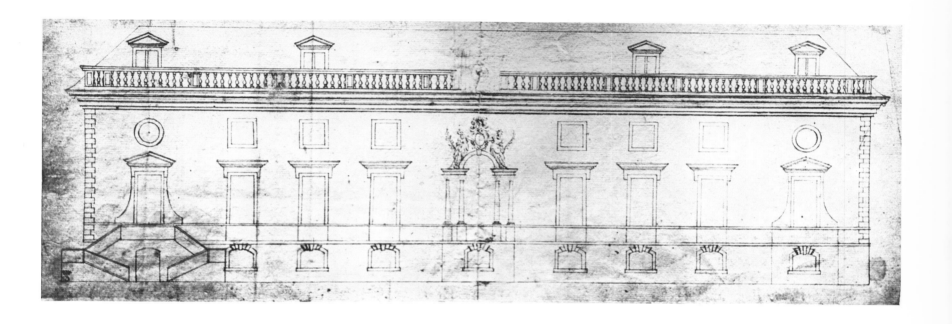

7. *John Webb (1611-1672)*
Design for the decoration of an unidentified room
Elevation, with measurements and numerations
Pen and faint touches of wash
Lit. & reprd. Oliver Hill & John Cornforth, *English Country Houses: Caroline 1625—1685*, 1966, figs 115/116
VICTORIA AND ALBERT MUSEUM

7b

7a

This design (7), and its companion (7a) for the inner side of an outer, that is entrance, wall, may well be for an entrance hall. The hand is Webb's, and the comparison of the design with the Single Cube Room at Wilton logically suggests an association with that house, especially now that it has been demonstrated that before the fire of 1647 both the Double and Single Cubes are likely to have had beamed ceilings above an attic, instead of the present coves. However, the size of this room, 30 feet square but only 24 feet 5 inches high, does not fit any room at Wilton and though one would have expected the birds to have been the Herbert Wyverns, they are not. Nevertheless, the drawings represent a rare survival of decoration in the court style of the later 1640s, concurrent with Webb's re/instatement programme at Wilton from 1649 onwards. Figure 7b shows the Single Cube Room at Wilton, adjacent to the Double Cube on the south front. The decoration is by Webb, the painted ceiling in the style of de Critz.

7: fo: 8 ̃ᵐ: from out to out of the mould.

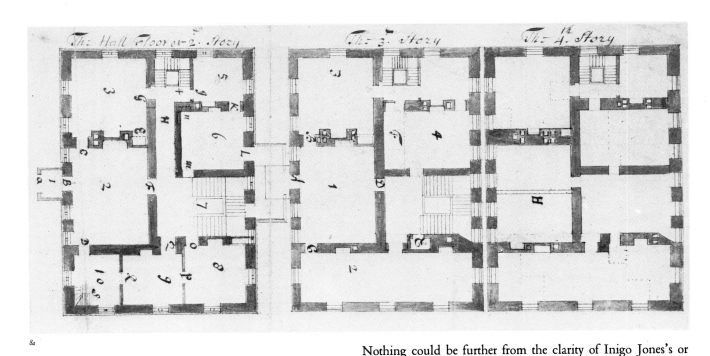

The Hall Floor or 2. Story   The 3. Story   The 4. Story

8a

Nothing could be further from the clarity of Inigo Jones's or John Webb's designs than this ungrammatical and muddled elevation that may be for a town house or one in the suburbs of London. There are perhaps hints here of an illiterate reading of Le Muet's *Maniere De Bien Bastir* of 1647 (Englished as *The Art of Fair Building* in 1670). Nevertheless, the elevations are characteristic of the robust, City of London style practiced by builders and bricklayers that permeated the Home Counties, especially Hertfordshire, between the late 1640s and c.1670. The floor plans (*8a*) show an interior disposition as muddled as the exterior.

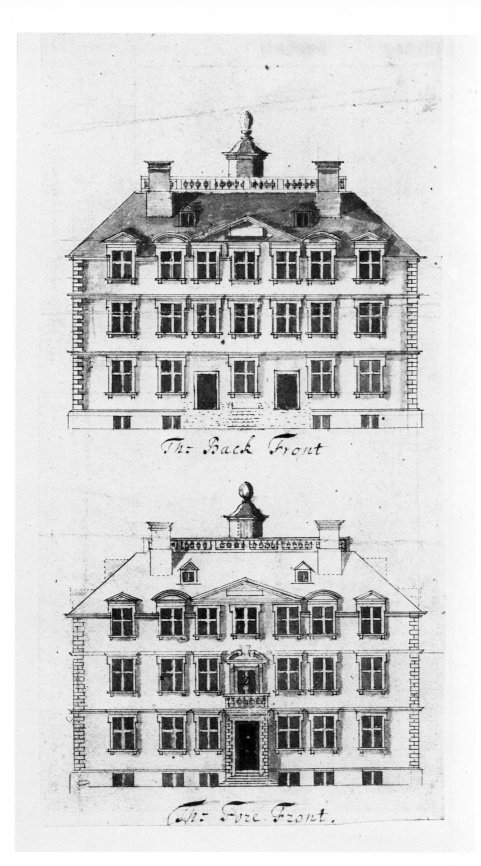

8. Anonymous English Architect c. 1650s
Design for a country house
Elevations of 'Back' and 'Fore' fronts
Pen and wash (226 x 118)
YALE CENTER FOR BRITISH ART,
PAUL MELLON COLLECTION

The Back Front

The Fore Front.

The association of this design with Easton Neston is tentative. It may relate to Sir William Fermor's planned building of about 1685, in which Wren was involved. The problems of the remodelling by Nicholas Hawkmoor some fifteen years later are outside the parameters of this entry, as is the matter of the wooden model—presumably by Hawksmoor, though possibly by Wren —preserved in the house. What we do have in this drawing is precious and rare evidence for Wren's prowess as a country house architect in the 1680s. In this design the parts that make up the pyramidal composition are arranged to provide a sense of movement. The attached French-styled frontispiece with superimposed pilasters links this design to the frontispieces pro-posed on the model that has always been in the house (9a). This model, possibly constructed in the early 1690s, proposes a somewhat squatter house, without the giant orders on the main front. In the matter of verticals and horizontals this is a more balanced design than the baroque verticality of the house as com-pleted in 1702 (9b shows the entrance front as built).

9a

9b

THE RESTORATION HOUSE

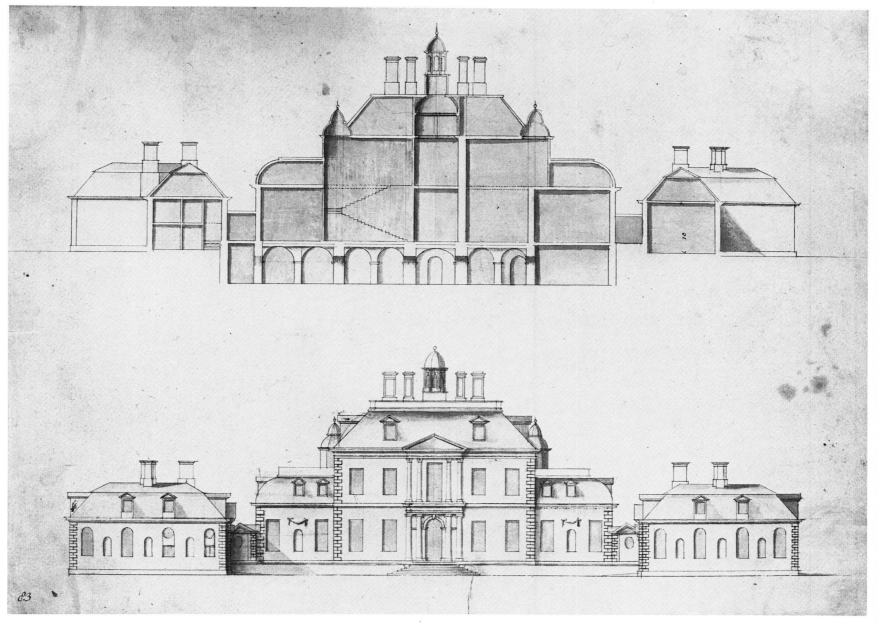

9. *Sir Christopher Wren (1632-1723)*
Easton Neston, Northamptonshire
Design for a new house
Elevation and section
Pencil, pen and wash (352 x 452)
Lit. & reprd. K. Downes, *Sir Christopher Wren*, Whitechapel
Art Gallery, London, 1982, pp 42-3, pl. I,11
THE WARDEN AND FELLOWS OF ALL SOULS, OXFORD

10a

This design comes from Wren's office and has been associated with the Queen's Closet at Hampton Court Palace, designed before 1694. It is characteristic of the fashion for carved wood decoration to chimney overmantels and to overdoors, and the drawing is almost certainly by Grinling Gibbons; the highly naturalistic fruit, flowers and birds in this particular design are in his best manner. It was ornament such as this, combined with painted ceilings, and often stucco-work, that distinguishes the decoration of rooms between about 1675 and the end of the century. Compare, for example, the State Drawing Room at Chatsworth House, Derbyshire (10a). The carving is by Samuel Watson, the Grinling Gibbons of Derbyshire, the ceiling painted by Antonio Verrio in about 1691, the tapestries are Mortlake after the Raphael cartoons, from the 1630s, the bolection chimney surround is of marble. Or there is Burghley House, Northamptonshire, the high point of William Talman's style: he was responsible for redecorations for the 5th Earl of Exeter in about 1688-90. Figure 10b shows an overdoor with complex and intricate carving attributed to Grinling Gibbons.

10b

10. *Sir Christopher Wren (1632-1723)* & *Grinling Gibbons (1648-1721)*
Hampton Court Palace, Middlesex
Design for the decoration of a chimney-piece and door, possibly for the Queen's closet
Elevation of one side of a wall showing a chimney-piece flanked by a door
Pen and pencil (360 x 420)
THE WARDEN AND FELLOWS OF ALL SOULS, OXFORD

THE RESTORATION HOUSE

11a

This design, for a room about 44ft by 32ft, is typical of plasterer's patterns after 1670. The scroll and ornamental work is deeply undercut and the foliage vigorously and naturalistically moulded. Such ceilings replaced the beam and cove system introduced by Inigo Jones, and would themselves be succeeded by the illusionistic Baroque ceilings made fashionable by pain- ters, such as Antonio Verrio, Louis Laguerre and Sir James Thornhill. Other ceilings attributed to Goudge are at Belton House in Lincolnshire, made between 1685 and 1688. Figure *11a* shows the ceiling of the staircase. The house was designed by William Winde and built by William Stanton for Sir John Brownlow between 1684 and 1687.

THE RESTORATION HOUSE

11. *Attributed to Edward Goudge (fl. 1680- about 1700)*
Design for a Restoration period ceiling
Plan, one quarter ornamented, with scale
Brown pen over pencil outline and some wash (355 x 245)
Lit. Geoffrey Beard, *Decorative Plasterwork in Great Britain*, 1975,
pp 48-50, 221
RIBA DRAWINGS COLLECTION

Stoke Edith House was one of the finest Williamite houses of the end of the 17th century. Celia Fiennes wrote in 1696 that Speaker or Auditor Paul Foley 'intends to make both a new house and gardens: the latter I saw staked out...' and in 1698 she saw the 'new house which was building'. The architect remains unknown, but this design came from the collection of Colen Campbell, being one of the designs acquired to be drawn and engraved for *Vitruvius Britannicus*, I, 1715, plates 45-6.

It is thus interesting that Campbell wrote that the house was 'designed and built' by Foley himself. In fact Foley died in 1697, so if he was an amateur architect he did not see the completion of his creation. Stoke Edith was built of brick with fine cut-stone dressings and ornamental stone work to the entrances (*12a* shows the west front facing the entrance courtyard), and with a hipped roof into which were set dormer windows. (The raised stone attic seen in *12b*, a view from the south-east, may be from about 1800 when C. H. Tatham made alterations for Edward Foley.) The house was also renowned for its magnificent painted mural decorations (*13*) by Sir James Thornhill, all tragically destroyed when Stoke Edith burnt down in 1927.

12a

12b

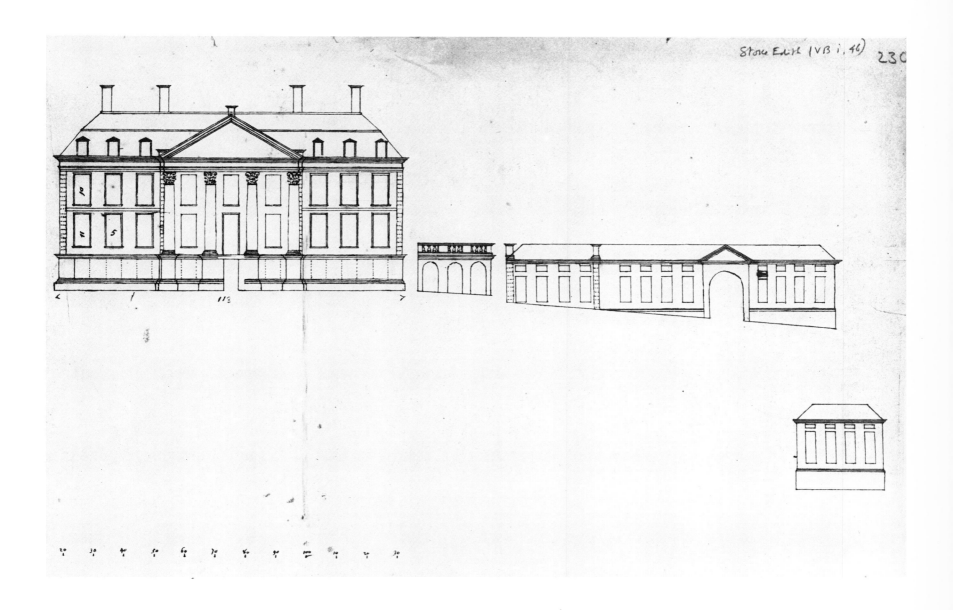

12. Unknown English Architect : possibly Paul Foley (died 1697)
Stoke Edith House, Herefordshire
Design for the north front
Elevation, with elevations of arcaded links and of ends of offices
to courtyard on west front, with scale
RIBA Drawings Collection

13b

13a

Although the design is typical of Thornhill, this drawing (*13*) is unique in his *oeuvre* both for its size and its finish, being closer in character to a finished oil study. More usual is such a design as *13b*, a vigorous sketch for Daniel Finch, 7th Earl of Winchelsea and 2nd Earl of Nottingham, for Eastwell Park, Kent, a late 16th or early 17th century house. The date may be about 1710, the subject Europa and the Bull. Thornhill's decoration can be admired in interiors such as the Great Hall at Stoke Edith (*13a*), one of the most splendid private halls in England,

a perfect example of what could be described as the 'bolection' style. The decorations by Thornhill were carried out for Thomas Foley (died 1737) and have been dated to about 1705. The theme chosen by Thornhill (or by Foley) was early Roman history. In the niche we see Liberty, and leaning upon the balustrade, Thomas Foley with Thornhill and a servant.

13. *Sir James Thornhill (1625-1734)*
Design for an unidentified staircase
Section showing elevation of upper
and under stair walls
Pen and wash, heightened with white
(530 x 470)
PRIVATE COLLECTION

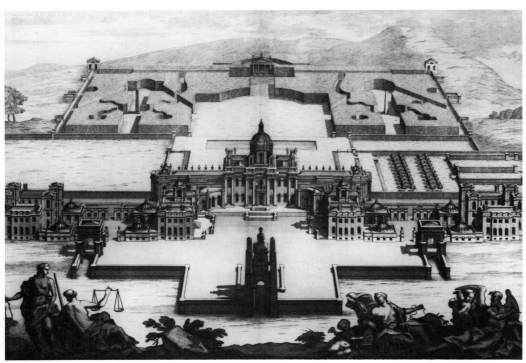

14a

14b

This is probably Vanbrugh's first or preliminary design for Castle Howard, drawn by Hawksmoor in about mid-1699, following the rejection of one by William Talman. It was the playwright-soldier, turned architect whose eye saw the scenic potential of turning the proposed Talman house around and spreading it across the ridge of the hill. As yet Vanbrugh's main block is relatively compressed, and the wings spread out lengthwise, connected to the main block only by single-story arcaded wings. In phase two the wings would be dramatically brought forward to make a deep forecourt, and progressively be built-up and made to be more integrated with the main block. With this design the great era of the English Baroque country house was initiated. Although some of Talman's designs can be described as Baroque, he, unlike Vanbrugh, was not concerned with the matter of volumetric mass, the play of mass against mass and the deliberate construction of shadowed contrasts. Indeed, Vanbrugh is pure theatre. Hawksmoor was his draughtsman and would later provide those ornamental roof-works called 'eminences'. The inscription on the drawing relates to the fact that the Duke of Newcastle had asked Vanbrugh for advice in 1703 about building a new house at Welbeck Abbey, Nottinghamshire, for which Talman had already supplied designs. In the hope of wresting the commission from Talman, Vanbrugh had obviously showed the Duke and his Duchess this design for Castle Howard as an example of his capabilities.

Although the perspective of Castle Howard (*14a*) was only published by Colen Campbell in the third volume of *Vitruvius Britannicus* in 1725, it conforms to the plan published in the second volume in 1717. While it is still unclear when either were invented, the perspective may be the working-up by Hawksmoor of a pen sketch made by Vanbrugh before 1710. The huge walled garden is certainly Vanbrugh's and contains an early example of the placing of a proper temple in a garden. The use of obelisks, likewise, in such a situation is also early, and there can be little doubt that this heroic ideal emerged out of concurrent experience of designing Blenheim Palace from 1705.

102   THE BAROQUE HOUSE

14. *Sir John Vanbrugh (1664–1736) & Nicholas Hawksmoor (c.1661–1736)*
Castle Howard, Yorkshire
Design for a new house
Elevation of entrance front seen in eye-level perspective
Insc. on verso by Margaret, Duchess of Newcastle *Mr. Vanbrook's draft of a great house*
Pen and grey washes (360 x 1060)
Lit. & reprd. Kerry Downes, *Vanbrugh*, 1977, pp 27-32, pl. 18, Jill Lever & Margaret Richardson,
The Art of the Architect, 1984, 50, pl 21
RIBA Drawings Collection

THE BAROQUE HOUSE

15b

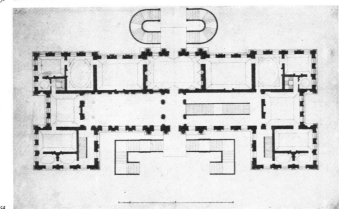

15a

Talman and Vanbrugh were in competition for the commission from the 1st Duke of Newcastle to rebuild old Welbeck Abbey in 1703, a contest that provoked much controversy and ill-feeling. Talman had almost certainly been approached first and had submitted a number of designs, not only for Welbeck, but also for the Duke's Haughton in the same county. Arrogant—for he was a man rich in his own right—Talman's demands and fees were frequently unacceptable, as they were for the Duke, who had already been approached by Vanbrugh, then obviously jubilant that Talman's lawsuit with Lord Carlisle over fees at Castle Howard had failed. In fact, Castle Howard spelt the end of Talman's dominance of the country house business. A new architecture was in the ascendant. Talman's was an eclectic style dependent upon a rich array of engraved sources, and in general his Welbeck design (15) could be described as text-book Franco-Italianate. For all that, the plan to Talman's Welbeck elevation (15a) demonstrates his ability as a planner of houses. In the case of this particular plan he had studied the Duke's great house at Nottingham Castle, built in the 1670s.

Compare one of Talman's many alternative designs for the Duke's house at Welbeck (15b), where his sources are bookish, in this case drawing upon both Rossi and Guarini, with the design (15c) spelt out by Vanbrugh in his own language, in response to Talman's pavilion composition.

15c

THE BAROQUE HOUSE

15. *William Talman (1650-1719)*
Welbeck Abbey, Nottinghamshire
Unexecuted design for rebuilding
Elevation of the garden front
Insc. Front 200 feet and, on verso (perhaps by the Duchess of
Newcastle) *One front of a house by Mr Tollman*
Pen & wash (220x320)
RIBA Drawings Collection

Front 200 feet

16b

16a

Kings Weston near Bristol, designed for Edward Southwell in 1712, represents a model of a country house by Vanbrugh quite independent of his associate Hawksmoor. Ornament is minimal, the effect is sombre and what matters is the mass, with the splendid pilastered portico and the majestic range of chimney stacks brought up together as a square of arcades. Vanbrugh sited the house on an eminence, and gave it four different fronts (16a shows the south or entrance front, 16b the east front). These other fronts were astylar, relying for their effect upon the proportioning of opening to wall, and their utilitarian character, an Office of Ordnance style translated into domestic use. The design or working drawing for the ground floor plan (16c), is also from Sir John Vanbrugh's office.

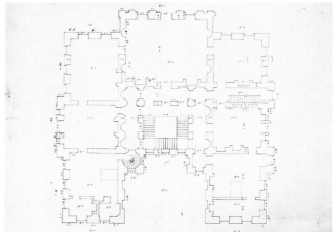

What is so fascinating and remarkable about Vanbrugh is that his scenic sense entered into the body of the house. His was no static plan, and although he had certainly learnt something from Talman's own spatially-constructed plans, his was a new system in which he was the first to exploit to the full the corridor. Grand his plans might be, but they were undoubtedly the most functional state rooms in Europe at that time, which in the Victorian age would be reverently admired.

THE BAROQUE HOUSE

16. *Sir John Vanbrugh (1664-1726)*
Kings Weston House, Gloucestershire
Design for a new house
Elevation
Brown ink & grey wash (368 x 470)
Lit. (for associated drawings), K. Downes, 'The Kings Weston
Book of Drawings', *Architectural History,* 10, 1967
YALE CENTER FOR BRITISH ART, PAUL MELLON
COLLECTION

THE BAROQUE HOUSE

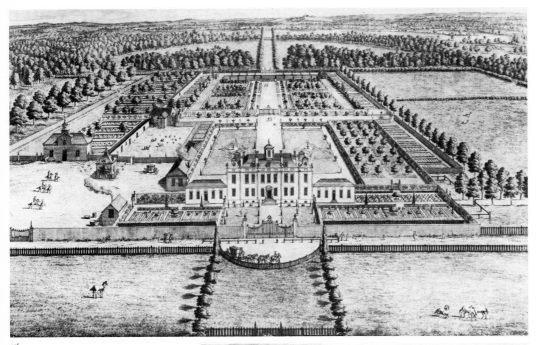

17b

17a

Although celebrated for its Italianate garden, the Evelyn family seat in Surrey was never more than a moderately sized manor house, adequate for a family who were never wealthy by the standards, for example, of Hawksmoor's patron, Lord Leominster of Easton Neston. The commission must surely have only been a passing whim of Sir John Evelyn's, for he could never have afforded the formidable expense of building such a design. Apart from Easton Neston, Hawksmoor was never given the opportunity of exercising his talents on country houses, in contrast to the many designed by Vanbrugh. It is therefore difficult to judge this design in such isolation. The design is notably astylar, and relies for its effect upon the advance, recession, and balance of planes. It might seem that Hawksmoor is here providing his own astylar answer to Vanbrugh's designs. Shorn of its roof-works this is a remarkably restrained design. Indeed, the pedimented towers, and notably the pedimented parts of the wings, are almost neo-Palladian, and thus the traditional dating of this project to August 1713 (when Sir John Evelyn records a visit to Wotton by Hawksmoor) should not be accepted without caution. However, Nicholas Hawksmoor's design for the side of the Evelyn house at Wotton (17a) is only lightly pencilled and ruled, the wash applied rather rudimentarily, almost as if Hawksmoor made the drawings on the spot at the behest of the owner.

John Kip's engraved view (17b) is of Sir Godfrey Kneller's house at Twickenham, known to have been built in about 1709, but still in search of an architect. There are resemblances between this and the Hawksmoor design, if only through a common Office of Works experience.

THE BAROQUE HOUSE

17. *Nicholas Hawksmoor (c.1661-1736)*
Wotton House, Surrey
Design for a new house
Elevation of entrance front
Insc (verso: since erased) *Upright S⸴ Ch⸴.*
Pen, pencil & wash (335 x 830)
RIBA DRAWINGS COLLECTION

18. Anonymous English Architect

18. Anonymous English Architect
Two designs for a large country house
(1) Elevation
Sepia ink on varnished paper stuck on card (190 x 320)
(2) Elevation, with scale
Pen and wash (100 x 200)
RIBA DRAWINGS COLLECTION

18b

Both designs (*18*) seem to be related, but are in different hands and it is not clear if they are for the same project. The smaller design proposes a house of 163 feet, the larger a house of comparable frontage. The designs owe an allegiance to those who favoured the use of the giant order. There are strong echoes in the larger design of Ince Blundell Hall, Lancashire, about 1715, and in the smaller of Wren's Marlborough House, London, 1709. Both represent the thoughts of a provincial architect responsive to London design, and they could be by John Price (died 1736), the architect of St George's Chapel, Yarmouth, who seems to have absorbed much of Wren and Talman.

The garden front of Ince Blundell, Lancashire, (*18a*) contains elements identifiable with some in the two unknown designs, while Wotton House, Buckinghamshire, about 1710, here (*18b*) drawn by Sir James Thornhill, was an early example of a type of house framed by a giant order and with an attic and attic pilasters, that became a popular model.

18a

THE BAROQUE HOUSE

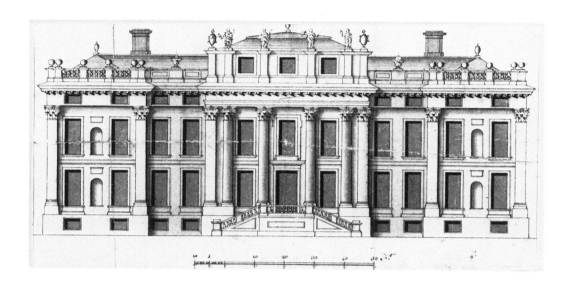

THE BAROQUE HOUSE

19c

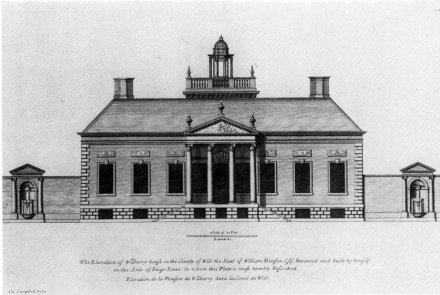

The Elevation of Wilbery house in the County of Wilt the Seat of William Benson Esq Invented and built by himself in the Stile of Inigo Jones, to whom this Plate is most humbly Inscribed.
Elevation de la Maison de Wilbery dans la Comté de Wilt.

19a   C. Campbell Delin.

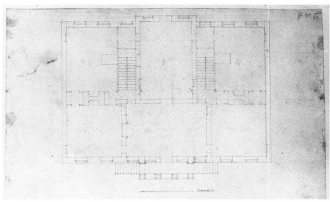

19b

Wilbury is the first neo-Palladian country house. William Benson, who had married in 1707, bought a lease of Amesbury Abbey, Wiltshire, John Webb's celebrated Palladian house. Less than a year later he bought land (without a house) nearby and began to build Wilbury. This elevation (19), drawn for Campbell's *Vitruvius Britannicus* I, 1715, (19a) comprises the top half of Amesbury laid upon a low basement. Although there is no documentary evidence, it is likely that Benson played some part in converting Colen Campbell to neo-Palladianism, for when in 1718 Benson acquired the Surveyorship of the Works, upon the dismissal of Wren, he made Campbell his Deputy.

Before 1708 there was no such place as Wilbury, and it must be assumed that Benson invented the name by adding the 'bury' of Amesbury to the 'Wil' of Wilton (also in Wiltshire), thus endowing his house with a name redolent of two houses believed to have been designed by the great Inigo Jones. Similarly, the plan of Wilbury, here (19b) as drawn for the engraver in *Vitruvius Britannicus*, I, 1715, is a blending of the plans of Palladio's Villa Sarego and Villa Pogliana.

Campbell's enthusiasm knew no bounds when it came to 'improving' many of the buildings presented in *Vitruvius Britannicus*. Although this topographical view (19c) is crudely drawn, it shows how Campbell improved the platform and cupola set over the back hall or saloon. Curiously, at Amesbury this type of tower had a specific function, to contain and light the stairs, but here it seems at odds with the plan.

19. William Benson (1682-1754)
Wilbury House, Wiltshire
Measured elevation of the entrance front, with scale
Insc. The Elevation of Wilberry House in the County of Wilts the Seat of W. Benson Esqr. Invented by himself
Pencil and pen (255 x 380)
Lit. & reprd. John Harris, *The Palladians*, 1981, pp 60-61, fig. 34
RIBA DRAWINGS COLLECTION

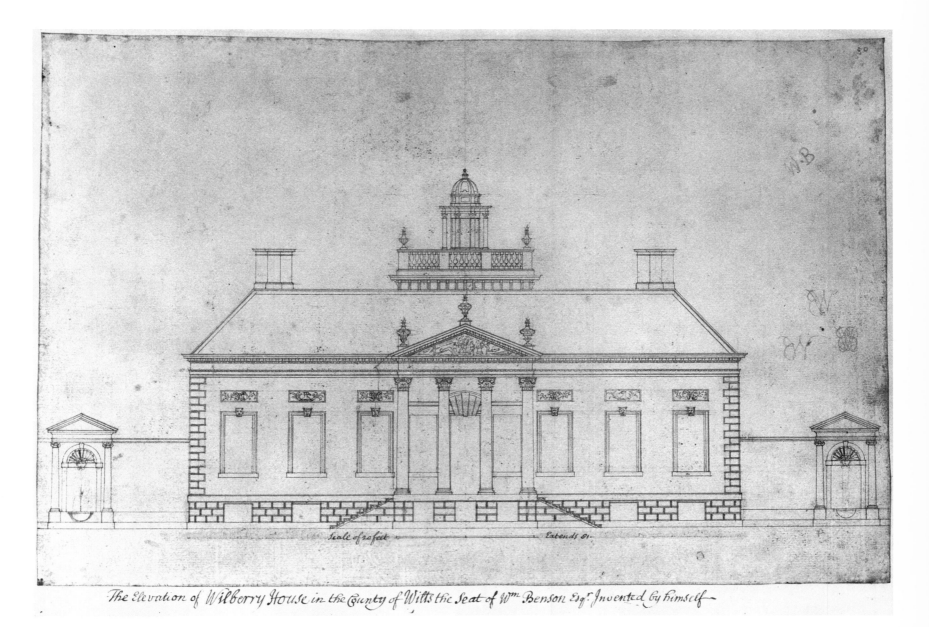

The Elevation of Wilberry House in the County of Wilts the Seat of Wm Benson Esqr Invented by himself

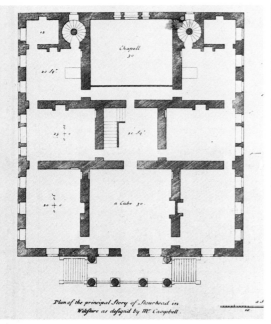

20a

20b

Although Stourhead, built from 1720 for Henry Hoare, was not Campbell's first villa, it was the one that attracted and received the most public attention, and thus became the archetypal model for neo-Palladian villas, not only for architects practising in the 1720s, but likewise for a later generation that included Ware, Chambers and Taylor (Campbell himself would adapt the Stourhead formula for Houghton in 1722 and at Plumptre House in 1724). Hoare's uncle was none less than William Benson of Wilbury, who may well have advised on the building as well as the laying-out of the gardens. For both plan and elevation Campbell chose Palladio's Villa Emo as his model (*20a* shows the plan from *Vitruvius Britannicus*, III, 1725). For the side elevations (*20b*) he paraphrased the garden front of his own Wanstead of 1713: although the front of the house (*20*) was of villa form with the windows arranged in one-three-one bays, Stourhead was not a secondary seat of the family, but Hoare's principal one, and thus was required to be larger than a Chiswick or a Mereworth.

20. Colen Campbell (1676-1729)
Stourhead, Wiltshire
Design for a new villa
Elevation of east or entrance front, with scale
Pen & wash (355 x 520)
Lit. & reprd. John Harris, *The Palladians*, 1981, p. 65, pl. 40
RIBA DRAWINGS COLLECTION

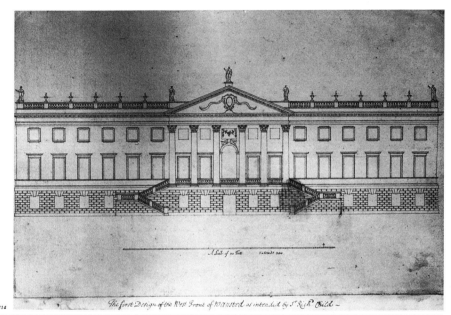

21a The first Design of the West Front of Wanstead as intended by S.r Rich.d Child

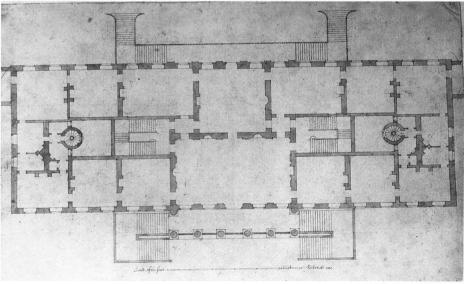

21b

This design (21), known in the typology of the great neo-Palladian country house as Wanstead One, was made in 1713 for Sir Richard Child. He had at this time finished laying out the magnificent gardens, begun in 1707 by George London, and was reported as being 'ready to build' in 1712. For him Campbell exploited the neo-Palladian style for the first time in his career. This huge unrelieved block must have appeared innovative as compared to what Vanbrugh was building in the Baroque style at exactly the same time. This design, prophetic of the new style, must surely have persuaded Campbell to neo-Palladianise *Vitruvius Britannicus*, the first volume of which was to appear in May, 1715, including both an elevation and ground floor plan of Wanstead One, the drawings for which are illustrated opposite (*21 a & b*). In this volume Palladio and Jones are Campbell's champions. Wanstead One was, in fact, Scamozzian, his engraved Villa Verlata from the *Idea della Architettura Universale*, 1615, spliced to the floor and bay arrangements that made up the elevation of the Jonesian Lindsey House, Lincolns Inn Fields, and Dr Aldrich's neo-Palladian Peckwater Quad, Christchurch, Oxford, of 1707. The portico was to exercise a formidable influence, notably upon Gibbs's St Martins in the Fields and on Lord Burlington's Chiswick Villa. It was the first proper temple-portico, for its ridge passed through the house to appear on the opposite front as a pilastered portico. Because Wanstead was sited on the edge of London it was a cynosure for the tourist's eye and therefore tremendously influential. (*21c* shows a detail of the garden front of Wanstead, drawn by George Robertson in the 1760s, presenting the powerful effect of ranges of voussoired windows with massive keystones and pediments.) The house was demolished in 1824.

21c

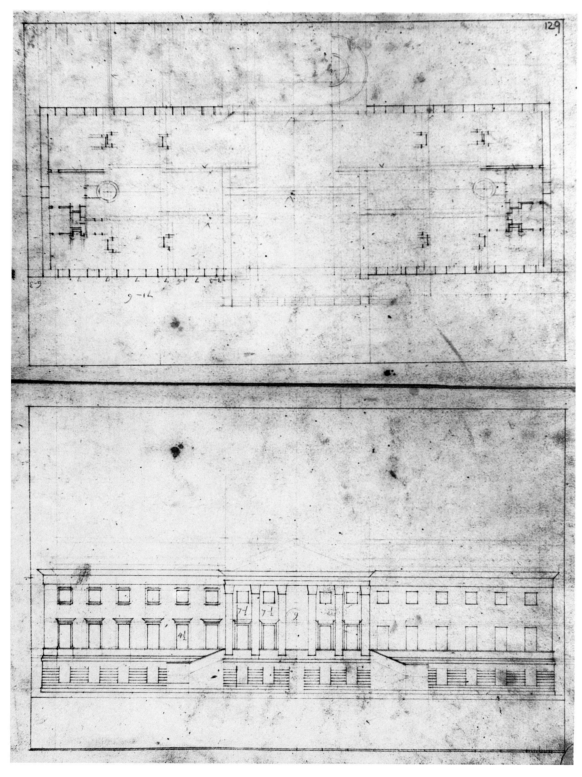

21. *Colen Campbell (1676-1729)*
Wanstead House, Essex
Design for a new house
Plan, and elevation of west front.
Signed & dated. CC *1713*
Pencil, pen and wash (585 x 440)
Lit. & reprd. John Harris, *RIBA Catalogue...*
Campbell, 1972, fig. 121; and John Harris,
The Palladians, 1981, pp 62-3
RIBA DRAWINGS COLLECTION

If Wanstead represents Campbell's solution to the problem of the 'Great House' at the beginning of his professional career, Houghton is his *beau-ideal* for such a house in his maturity, ten years on. It was begun for Sir Robert Walpole in 1722, although Campbell's first designs (*22*) are dated only 1723, and were then drastically modified. As this design demonstrates, Campbell was fond of using voussoired openings: the voussoired Palladian window was his speciality, as were the octagonal lanterns, proposed on this design and used to crown the stables. This first design is closest of all Campbell's versions to the great prototype at Wilton, to the extent of the central window (lifted from the south front) and the auricular-looking oval windows in the towers (taken from Isaac de Caus's grotto building in the gardens). *22a* shows Houghton as designed by Campbell with Wilton-style towers, probably in 1723-24: the portico on this entrance front is a full one, but as built, was pulled back and attached. Also, Campbell's first plan for the ground floor of the Wilton-tower model, (*22b*), although a traditional double-pile type with saloon and hall on axis, was made remarkable by the neo-Palladian hall, a 40 foot cube with gallery based upon Jones's famous prototype at Greenwich.

Houghton has always been regarded as the best model of a neo-Palladian tower house, evoking the south front of Wilton, but this judgement requires modification, for this 'tower house' as published by Campbell in *Vitruvius Britannicus* III, 1725, was not built with towers, but with an undistinguished hipped roof. The present domed terminations of the towers were added by James Gibbs in about 1727 (*22c* shows Humphry Prideaux's view of the house while they were building).

22a

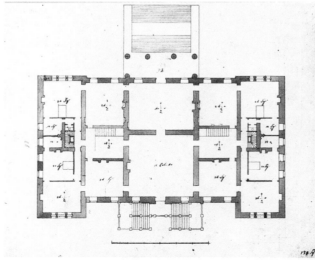

22b

Houghton At Hon Sr Robt Walpole. Norfolk

22c

22. Colen Campbell (1676-1729)
Houghton Hall, Norfolk
Design for the west or court front
Elevation with scale.
Insc. (verso, by Campbell) The first Design of
the Court front of Houghton 1723 C:C:
Pen and wash (310 x 500)
RIBA DRAWINGS COLLECTION

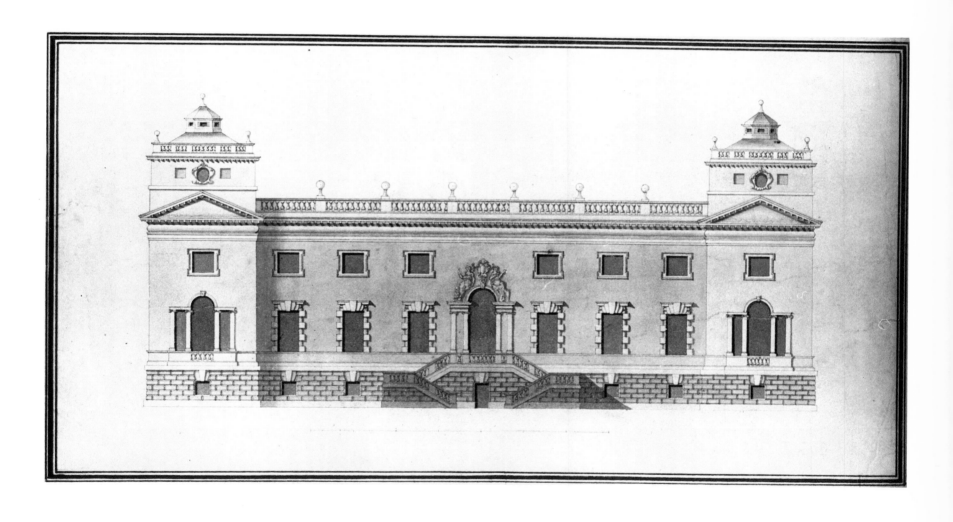

THE NEO-PALLADIAN HOUSE

Campbell proudly published Mereworth in *Vitruvius Britannicus*, III, 1725, and as he mentions roofing in 1723, it must therefore have been designed about 1721. The inspiration to place on English soil a version of Palladio's Villa Capra or Rotonda may not have been Campbell's own, for one of the designs is inscribed in 'Vicentine feet' in a hand suspiciously like Lord Burlington's. Campbell experimented with many designs, some large, some small, before deciding upon a plan measuring 90 feet square, compared to the 80 feet square of the Rotonda. Whereas the Rotonda stands upon a hill, four square to the countryside, Mereworth is on the flat, but when built was surrounded by a moat so that the two porticoes formed as loggias were reflected in the water, a most felicitous idea (*23a* shows the house as it is today, the moat filled in). The main difference between the planning of Mereworth to that of the Rotonda is the more convenient domestic arrangements, with suites of rooms only broken by an access passage on one front. Mereworth also marked an innovation in chimney flue design, in that the flues were brought up between the outer and inner shells of the dome to exit at the cupola.

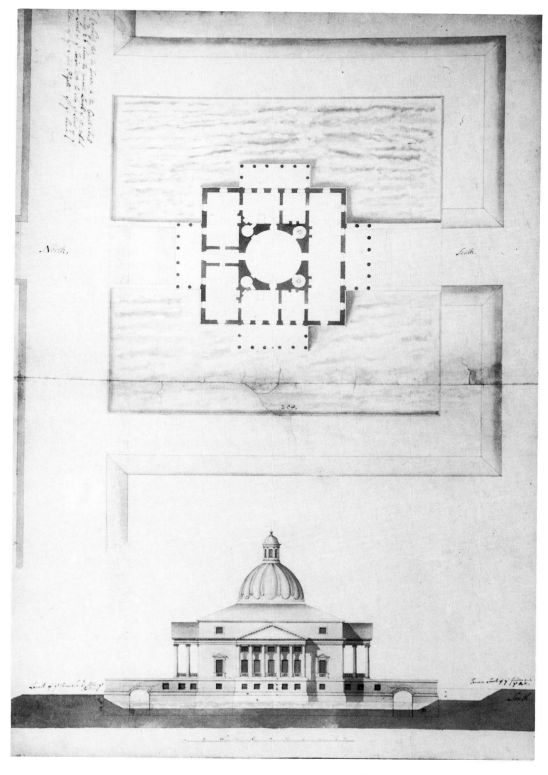

22. Colen Campbell (1676-1729)
Mereworth Castle, Kent
Design for a rotonda villa
Plan of site with ground floor plan and elevation, with section
through moat and with scale
Pen & wash (730 x 510)
Lit. & reprd. John Harris, *The Palladians*, 1981, p. 66, pl. 42
RIBA Drawings Collection

THE NEO-PALLADIAN HOUSE

By 1721 Stourhead and Burlington House, London, had made Campbell the premier professional neo-Palladian architect. He was soon to be challenged, for in 1720 Lord Burlington had entered the lists with Tottenham House, Wiltshire, to be followed with the much published Westminster Dormitory. There was now no doubt as to what a neo-Palladian exterior should look like, but it was quite another matter with interiors. Campbell naturally looked to the Jonesian (by John Webb) Double Cube Room at Wilton, and his compositions of fruit and so on hanging from masks come from that source. There are other sources, notably in Palladio's woodcuts, or it was a matter of bringing external elements indoors. At Burlington House the putti sitting upon the Saloon doorcases come from the windows of Palladio's Palazzo Chiericati, and here at Mereworth (24) the head set in front of a shell also comes from that town house. At Mereworth, again, in the central hall beneath the dome, completed about 1726 (24a), the arched entrances with their ceiling figures are lifted directly from De Caus's central window on the south front of Wilton. Campbell's problem was the scarcity of complete, proper Palladian or Jonesian interiors, although it might be more true to say that Campbell did not bother to make a study of what was available. He might have examined, for example, the beam system of the Banqueting House, the interiors at the Queen's House, and the splendid Jonesian interiors at Webb's Gunnersbury, so near London; indeed, any of the Jonesian houses that he had published! As Lord Burlington would soon demonstrate, Campbell never understood that the grammar of Jones's interiors was to be found in Palladio's fourth book, on Roman antiquity.

24. *Colen Campbell (1676-1729)*
Mereworth Castle, Kent
Preliminary design for the interior
Section, with scale
Pen and wash (330 x 465)
Lit. & reprd. John Harris *RIBA Catalogue Campbell*, p. 141
fig 94
RIBA Drawings Collection

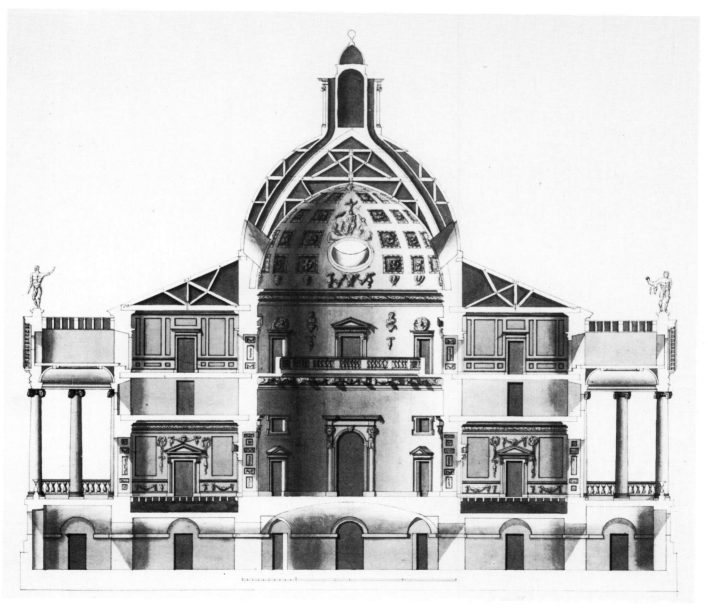

THE NEO-PALLADIAN HOUSE

The two buildings that are pre-eminent in Burlington's career are Tottenham and Chiswick, and they represent a beginning and an end, two polarities in the grammar and assemblage of architecture. Tottenham was his testing ground, the first work in his career as the Architect Earl, and it is not surprising that more designs for Tottenham survive than for any other building, his own Chiswick not excepted. Burlington's method was still that of Campbell: borrowing from the known works of Inigo Jones and from the woodcuts in Palladio's *Quattro Libri*. The

triumphantly used when assembling Chiswick in 1724.

Lord Burlington's design for the garden or park front of Tottenham (*25a*) may appear to be concurrent with the entrance front, but it is not, being almost certainly designed about 1727 when a front was added on the park, thus making Tottenham into a proper Palladian tower house. The strange portico—perhaps a viewing platform for the game in the park—is taken directly from Jones's loggia at the Queen's House. There is evidence that this may have been attached to the 1721 house, as

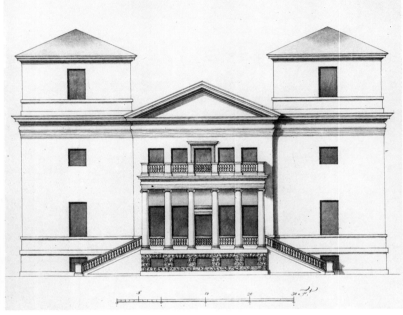

25b

25a

sources that can be identified in Tottenham as evolved from the beginning of building works in 1720 are Webb's Gunnersbury House, Middlesex, for a preliminary plan and the stairs, adapted and modified, from Palladio's villa for Annibale Sarego. At the same time the elevation for the free-standing kitchen wings was taken from Palladio's Villa Pogliana. For this entrance front, the recessed part and the steps are taken from the back of Gunnersbury, (therefore studied by Burlington on the spot), whereas the central tower is from Webb's Amesbury. Other sources are to be identified, notably the tower-house idea inspired by the famous south front of Wilton, and a staircase design based upon Coleshill House, Berkshire, then also believed to be a master-work of Inigo Jones, as was Gunnersbury and Amesbury. All this type of borrowing would soon change, for having acquired the original designs by Jones, Webb and Palladio in 1720 and 1721, Burlington discovered a wholly unexpected source for a grammar of architecture, one that he

this mode of borrowing is very definitely pre-1725 rather than post.

This early 19th-century watercolour (*25b*) was made by John Buckler shortly before Thomas Cundy enlarged and remodelled the house for the 1st Marquess of Ailesbury. The Burlington house of the 1720s had added to it four wings designed by Burlington in 1737, making Tottenham into a mininature Holkham. These wings were in turn influenced by Burlington's Link Building at Chiswick, added in 1733. Thus Tottenham in this Buckler view represents the gamut of Burlington's architectural career and development.

THE NEO-PALLADIAN HOUSE

25. *Richard Boyle, 3rd Earl of Burlington (1694-1753) & Henry Flitcroft (1697-1769)*
Tottenham Park, Wiltshire
Design for the east or entrance front
Elevation, with scale
Signed & dated. 1721 Burlington Ar:
Pen and wash (215 x 225)
Lit. & reprd. John Harris, 'The Building Works of Lord Viscount Bruce', *Lord Burlington and His Circle*, Georgian Group Symposium 1982, pp 25-51, fig 9
TRUSTEES OF THE CHATSWORTH SETTLEMENT

THE NEO-PALLADIAN HOUSE

As has been explained above (25) Tottenham Park, Wiltshire, had been built for Lord Burlington's brother-in-law, Lord Bruce, as Burlington's first essay as an architect in his own right and is Campbellian in assembly. When he began to design his own house at Chiswick in 1724 everything was different, and he now sought authority for every part in original drawings by Jones, Webb and Palladio, in Palladio's reconstructions of Roman antiquity bought in 1719, in Palladio's famous book and in Antoine Desgodetz's *Edifices Antiques de Rome* of 1682, the standard printed work on Roman antiquity. No building

26c

26b

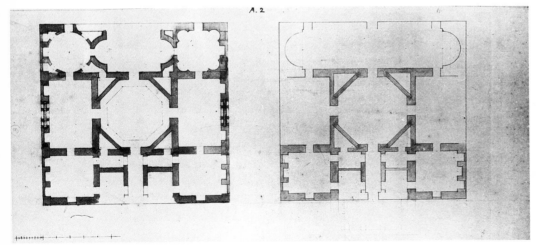

26a

an impression increased by the details and ornamentation, all of which come from the Corinthian order.

Although Chiswick (26) was admired and much visited, curiously it was never directly used as a model, but became a rich storehouse for architects and designers to plunder for parts of architecture. The manner in which Burlington built up his plan from Roman antiquity, and the perhaps conscious thought that he was doing what Pliny might have done, makes Burlington the first Neoclassical architect.

This elevation (26) was redrawn for Burlington by Henry Flitcroft. 26a, a design for the ground or undercroft floor of Chiswick, is his own roughly-rendered drawing, which would also have been immaculately redrawn by Flitcroft. Clearly Burlington was not a professional draughtsman; for example, he lacked the ablity to colour in an outline plan with wash, precisely and without spreading over the lines.

By the end of 1733 Burlington had been compelled to use the old house and the new villa in tandem, and to this end designed the Link Building. In this detail from J.F. Rigaud's view of Chiswick (26b) the old house is shown with the frontispiece added by Burlington about 1721. A recut of an engraving by J. Rocque dated 1736 (26c) shows the garden side of the villa with the Link Building, between it and a free-standing room, the Summer Parlour, of indeterminate date.

in Europe reflects such an obsession with authority, and although Chiswick is remarkable for this very fact, it is rendered not a little pedantic by such an obsession. The source in Palladio's Villa Rotonda is obvious, but a comparison with Mereworth Castle, that other villa modelled on the Rotonda, demonstrates how warming and attractive Mereworth is compared to the clinical, cerebral effect of Chiswick. Its small size and the way it seems polished by authority render it jewel-like,

THE NEO-PALLADIAN HOUSE

26. Richard Boyle, 3rd Earl of Burlington (1694-1753) & Henry Flitcroft (1697-1769)
Chiswick House, Middlesex
Design for the south or entrance front
Elevation, with scale
Pen and wash (310 x 370)
Lit. & reprd. John Harris, *The Palladians*, 1981. pp 74-75, pl. 57
RIBA DRAWINGS COLLECTION

This section is cut through the rooms on the west side of the Villa: from left to right, the Blue Velvet Room, the Red Velvet Room and the West Gallery Tribune. A study of the decoration of these rooms demonstrates Lord Burlington's fanatical search for authority in ancient and modern architecture, for the source of almost every detail can be located, if not in the Corinthian order as published by Palladio in his *Book One*, then in Palladio's *Book Four*, or Desgodetz's *Edifices Antiques de Rome*. In addition, chimney-pieces were constructed from original designs

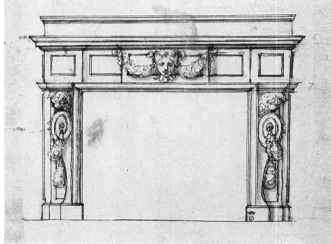

by Inigo Jones, usually by taking a chimney surround and marrying it to a chimney overmantel from another design (three designs that were used on the *piano nobile* at Chiswick are illustrated in *27 a,b,c*). More esoteric precedents can be located in other drawings that Lord Burlington owned, notably a design in the manner of Guilio Romano for a double-consoled ceiling, as in the Ducal Palace and the Palazzo del Té in Mantua, that served for the Blue Velvet Room. This section (drawn by Henry Flitcroft) must have been prepared about 1730, and it was probably Burlington's intention to produce a set of engravings of Chiswick. In the event only the plan and exterior were engraved in bistre wash in an edition limited to a few copies.

27a

27b

27c

THE NEO-PALLADIAN HOUSE

27. *Richard Boyle, 3rd Earl of Burlington & Henry Flitcroft*
Chiswick House, Middlesex
Section from south (left) to north through villa on west side
Pen and wash (345 x 445)
Lit. & reprd. John Harris, *The Palladians*, 1981, p.123, pl. 150.
TRUSTEES OF THE CHATSWORTH SETTLEMENT

28a

28b

Thomas Coke's wish for a new, fashionable country house must obviously date from as early as his Grand Tour, in Italy before 1720, but proof of any initiative can only be found from 1725/26, when Colen Campbell was paid 16 guineas, a sum about right for a set of designs. At this time, also, Mattthew Brettingham, soon to be the Holkham clerk of the works, was paid 10 guineas 'for drawing a Plan of a New House'. However, it was only in 1731 that the proper neo-Palladian tower house was in the making, and not until 1733 that the foundations were laid for the wings, though it may well be that a tower-house with wings was only conceived after 1731. In its planning, treatment of elevations and decoration, Holkham is the embodiment of the Burlington-Chiswick style, and can be seen as resulting from a round-table discussion between Burlington, Kent and Coke, the last-named an amateur of great distinction, who, though there is no evidence of his drafting ability, was virtually an architect in his own right. So pervading is the spirit of Chiswick and the York Assembly Rooms (built in 1731) that Burlington's authority cannot be doubted, and it was through Kent that he achieved Holkham as his ideal of the greater country house.

Kent's method of exterior composition as exemplified in this elevation has been aptly described as 'concatenated' or 'staccato', thus describing the advance and recession of planes and the breaking-up of the elevation and its dependent parts into units of various widths. The manner in which the wings are joined to the main block can be paralleled by the joining of the Link Building at Chiswick to the Villa, also effected in 1733. Concatenation enabled an elevation to be lengthened or shortened at will by the addition or subtraction of units. *28* is Kent's design for a stone-faced house, his 'best school of rusticks' style, *28a* is the front as built in bricks made locally, perhaps copying ancient Roman practice, and *28b* is the plan of the *piano nobile* floor of Holkam.

THE NEO-PALLADIAN HOUSE

28. William Kent (1686-1748)
Holkham Hall, Norfolk
Design for new house, showing treatment of rustication
Elevation of south front with free-hand sketch of woman
in classical dress leaning on an urn, with scale
Pen & wash (310 x 470)
Lit. R. Wittkower, 'Lord Burlington and William Kent',
Archaeological Journal, CII, 1945
TRUSTEES OF THE HOLKHAM ESTATE

As with so much else, at Chiswick and at York, and by 1733 probably also at Richmond Palace, and in their projects for the Houses of Parliament, Burlington and Kent turned to Roman antiquity, as presented by Palladio in his Fourth Book. *29a* shows a detail of the ceiling around the apsed end of the Great Hall, demonstrating Kent's use of Palladio's Fourth Book, as well as ornament from Desgodetz's *Les Edifices Antiques de Rome*, 1682. The plan that provided the first idea for this hall was that of the Temple of Venus and Roma, but set inside this was a theatrical encircling collonade, owing something to the Vitruvian-Palladian basilica in the Barbaro *Vitruvius*, and perhaps also a recollection of the open apsed screen of columns in the Chiesa del Redentore. The result is a piece of theatre, just as is Kent's staircase in 44 Berkeley Square, and it can hardly be disputed that there is no more innovative hall in the whole of the European renaissance. To those scholars who claim for Matthew Brettingham authority and originality at Holkham, one need only say, 'go to see Gunton Hall of 1742 and Euston Hall of 1750 to judge Brettingham's worth'.

THE NEO-PALLADIAN HOUSE

29. *William Kent (1686-1748)*
Holkham Hall, Norfolk
Design for the Great Hall
Plan, with three laid-back wall elevations and plan of ceiling,
with scale
Insc. by Kent, with various measurements
Pen & wash (335 x 500)
Lit. R. Wittkower, 'Lord Burlington and William Kent',
Archaeological Journal, CII, 1945
Trustees of the Holkham Estate

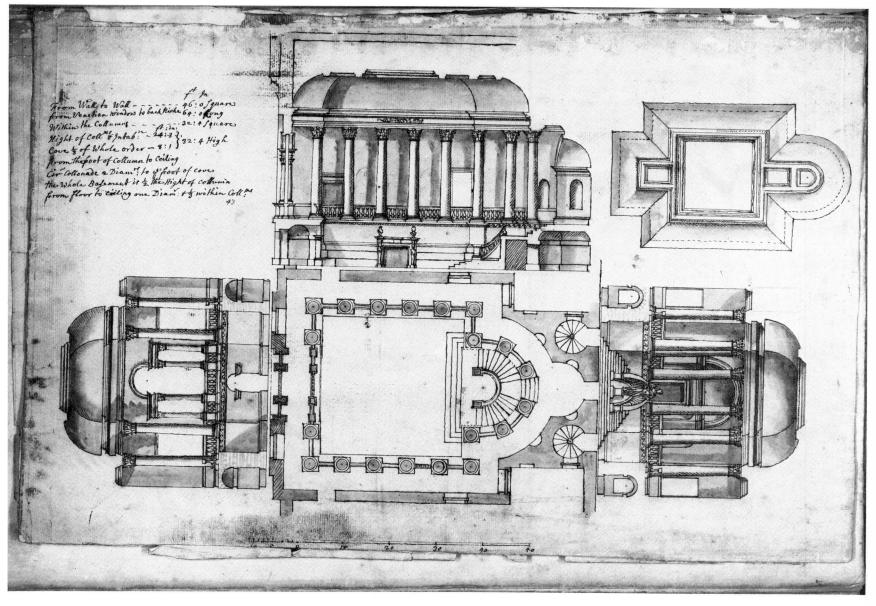

THE NEO-PALLADIAN HOUSE

Clues to the identification of this design (30) and its commission rest upon the size of the room, 36 by 26 feet, the military character of the ceiling and cove decorations, and the fact that the room was obviously a hall. Among Kent's patrons and friends is numbered Lord Cobham, who distinguished himself under Marlborough, and indeed this is the design for the north hall of Stowe, where in the centre of the ceiling Lord Cobham

receives a sword from Mars, amid panels of military trophies, and the cove has scroll-work incorporating military trophies and with medallion busts emblematic of the Zodiac. The chimney-piece shown in this design was not the one executed, as can be demonstrated by a comparison with Kent's design, (30a) also at Yale, and with the engraving of the actual chimney-piece in Isaac Ware's *Designs of Inigo Jones and others* about 1731, (plate 48) which shows the splendid bas-relief by Christophe Veyrier of the *Family of Darius before Alexander*, a relief that survives in the hall of Stowe today but without the chimney-piece. 30b

shows the north hall at Stowe, photographed before the sale of the contents of the house.

Kent's commission is undated, but must be from the late 1720s. Indeed it probably stands at the watershed between Kent the interior decorator and Kent the architect. The drawing characterises Kent's technique: a draughtsman supplies the outline framework, over which Kent makes loose, freehand sketches in his peculiar bistre-wash technique. Kent may be one of the first architects to present designs for a room in this novel 'laid-back' manner.

THE NEO-PALLADIAN HOUSE

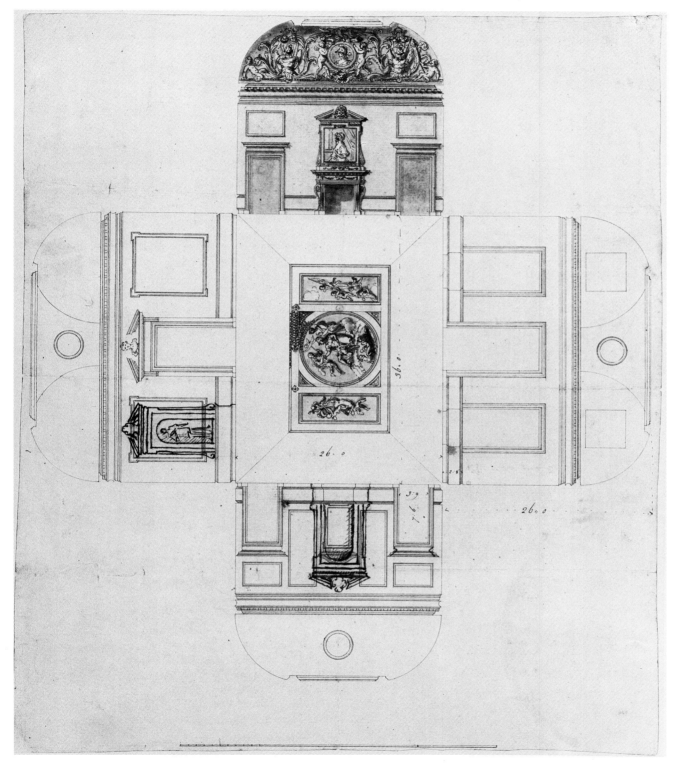

30. *William Kent (1686-1748)*
Stowe House, Buckinghamshire
Design for the decoration of the north
hall
Laid-back wall elevations with ceil-
ing plan, with scale
Pen and wash (388 x 320)
Lit. Edward Croft-Murray, *Decora-
tive Painting in England*, II, 1970, 235
YALE CENTER FOR BRITISH ART,
PAUL MELLON COLLECTION

Kent's Gothick (with a *k*) has been termed associational gothic because it was always built as an addition to an older Gothic, or usually Tudor, building. It is thus a style sympathetic to the earlier one, and Wren's completion of Tom Tower, Christ Church, Oxford, in 1681 is an early example. Kent's principal Gothick works for domestic accommodation are his additions to Hampton Court Palace, Middlesex, 1732, Esher Place, Surrey, 1733, Laughton Place, Sussex, about the same date, and Rousham House, Oxfordshire, 1738. All were originally buildings of Tudor date. Honingham Hall, an East Anglian crow-step gabled house built by Sir Thomas Richardson about 1605, was in 1737 (the year Kent dated the cover of the vellum album) in the possession of the Hon. William Townsend. Townsend was a likely patron for Kent, for not only was he the third son of the 2nd Viscount Townsend of Raynham Hall, Norfolk, where Kent had been engaged on large works from 1731, but he was also a Groom of the Bedchamber to Frederick, Prince of Wales. The fact that Kent dates this design on the verso *1738* is surprising, for Townsend died suddenly on 29 January of that year. This particular elevation is, however, a revised one, proposing a more extensive rebuilding. It must, therefore, have been made for Townsend's son Charles, Lord Bayning. Honingham never was rebuilt and was demolished in 1967.

The whole project is remarkably like that carried out later in the year at Rousham for General Dormer, and the abandoned Norfolk project must immediately have been taken up in Oxfordshire. The flanking offices, although Gothick in detail, are handled in Kent's special concatenated style. As we can see from *31a*, William Kent's detailed design for the porch at Esher Place, Surrey, signed and dated 1733, his grammar of Gothick ornament was uncomplicated, and often mixed with classical details, for example in the Greek key friezes to the capitals on the clustered shafts.

31. William Kent (1686-1748)
Honingham Hall, Norfolk
Unexecuted design for Gothickising the older house
Elevation with scale
Pen, pencil and wash (330 x 490)
Insc (verso) *for Honningham in Norfolk Wm Kent 1738*
Lit. J.J. Sambrook, 'Honingham Hall, Norfolk', *Norfolk
Archaeology*, XXXIV, pt III, 1968, pp 303-13
RIBA DRAWINGS COLLECTION

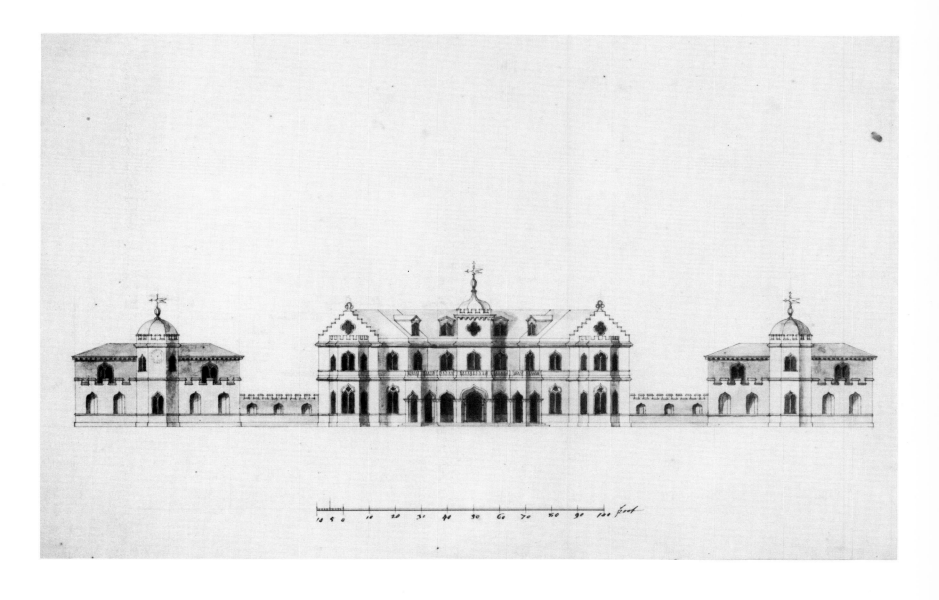

32a

Kent's Gothick is almost rudimentary, and in the designing of this Great Hall there is no attempt to transpose the spatial innovations of his classic planning into Gothick, or indeed to understand Gothic spatiality. Kent's Gothick is unlearned, but that is its charm. The same can be said of the Saloon at Rousham, Oxfordshire, about 1739-40 (*32a*), an epitome of Kent's mixing of Gothick and Classical styles to be seen both in the composition of the ceiling and the chimney surround.

32. William Kent (1686-1748)
Honingham Hall, Norfolk
Design for the decoration of the entrance hall
Plan with laid-back wall elevations, with scale
Pen, pencil and sepia wash (350 x 495)
Lit. Sambrook, *op. cit.*
RIBA DRAWINGS COLLECTION

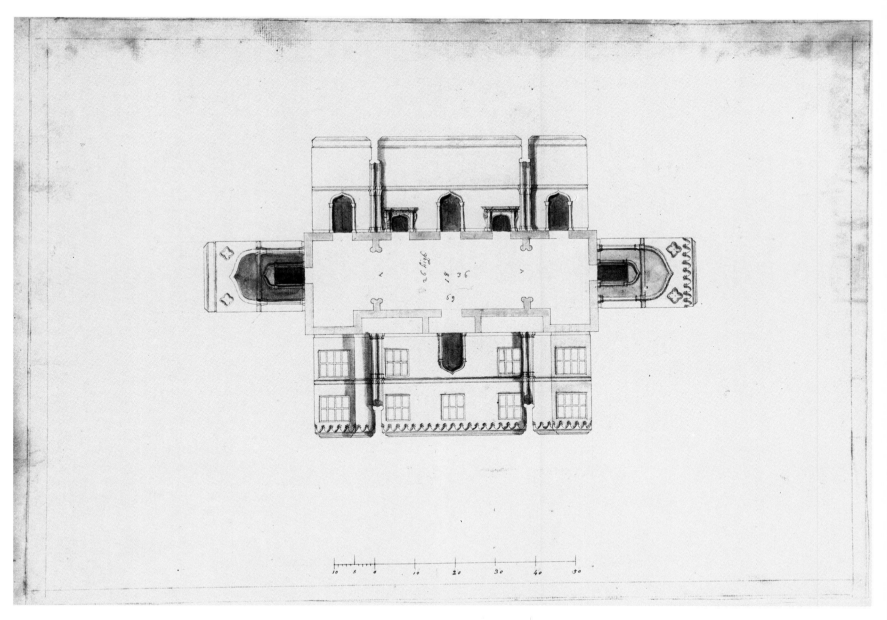

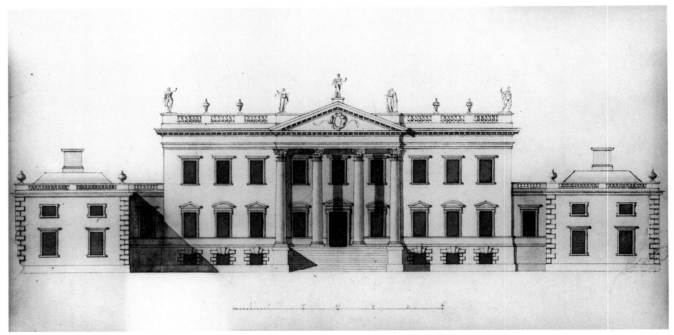

33a

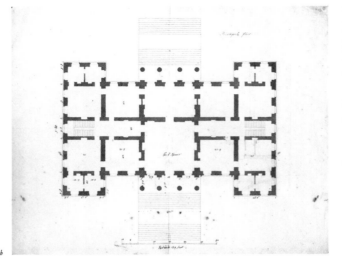

33b

This unexecuted design (*33*) is characteristic of the School of Baroque Compromise. Made after the Lowther fire of 1717, it is typical of his style in general, with complex mouldings, lugged frames and bracketted cornices. Pedestals are panelled and the piers between the balustrades are of complex outline. Gibbs's application of coloured wash is shadowed and warming, unlike Campbell's neo-Palladian cold grey tones. *33a* is a contrast to Gibbs's architecture of Baroque Compromise, being Campbell's design for the same house. It is markedly neo-Palladian, clean of line, minimal in colour, smooth and chaste, eschewing fussy ornamental detail. *33b* is Gibbs's plan for Lowther.

33. James Gibbs (1682-1754)
Lowther Hall, Westmorland
Design for rebuilding
Elevation of entrance front, with scale
Pen and wash (350 x 510)
Lit. & reprd. H.M. Colvin, J.M. Crook & T. Friedman, 'Architectural Drawings from Lowther
Castle Westmorland', *Architectural History Monographs*, 2, 1980, pp 4-7, 14-26, pl. 9a
RIBA DRAWINGS COLLECTION

Principale Front

34d

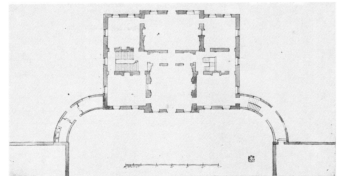

34b

Gibbs built Kelmarsh for William Hanbury from 1728: the rainwater heads are dated 1732. Not a grand house, rather reti-cent and built in red brick. This design for the saloon charac-terises the difference between the authoritative neo-Palladian decoration of Lord Burlington and Gibbs's own middle-of-the-road style, in this case relying for effect upon his stuccoists. Although there are hints, in the wall frames and the dependent swags, of the Double Cube Room at Wilton, no one detail is vested in either Jones or Palladio. As built (34a) the Hall at Kelmarsh was modified in the execution, notably substituting a beamed ceiling for the vaulted one, and later neo-Georgianised. Only the upper half and the ceiling retain Gibbs's design. 34b is the ground floor plan of Kelmarsh. The saloon is the room on the garden front with corridor between it and the hall. The design as published in his *Book of Architecture*, 1728, (34c) is somewhat grander. The house today (34d) is a villa in size, but with a front in Gibbs's favoured bay ratio of 2-3-2.

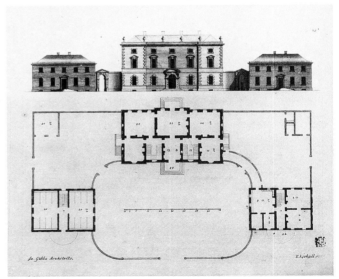

34c

34a

THE NEO-PALLADIAN HOUSE

34. James Gibbs (1682-1754)
Kelmarsh Hall, Northamptonshire
Design for the decoration of the saloon
3 wall elevations and plan of ceiling on one sheet, with scale
Insc. as for wall positions
Pen over pencil (420 x 505)
Lit. & reprd. Terry Friedman, *James Gibbs*, 1984, pp 125-26, 318, pl. 127
RIBA DRAWINGS COLLECTION

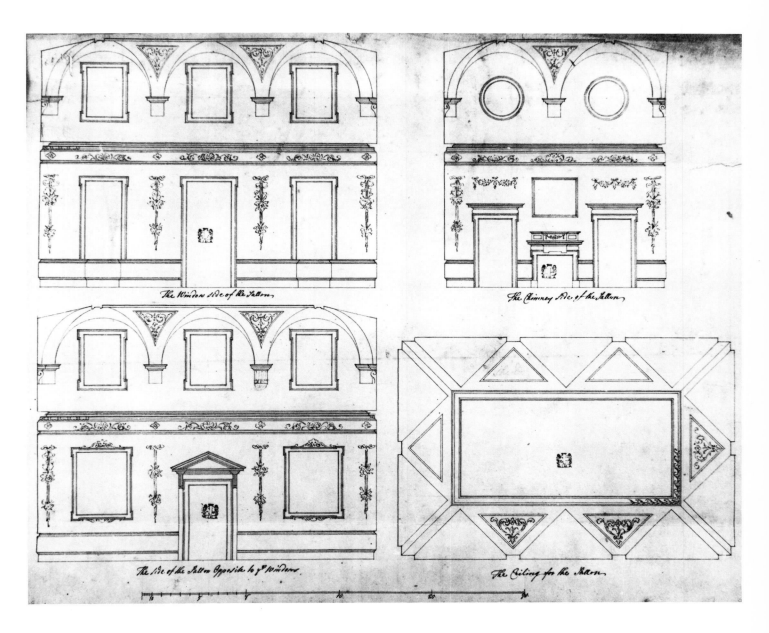

The Window side of the Saloon

The Chimney Side of the Saloon

The Side of the Saloon Opposite to ye Windows

The Ceiling for the Saloon

35a

35b

Whitton was designed for the Earl of Ilay, afterwards 3rd Duke of Argyll in about 1732, subsequent to the laying-out of part of Hounslow Heath as a nursery and aboretum, with James Gibbs as architect for the greenhouse seven years earlier. It was Morris who was favoured by Lord Ilay when that Earl decided to extend his nursery into a small garden with a dwelling house, long canal, and an ornamental Gothick tower (35a shows William Woollett's view of the house as built, in the 1750s). Whitton represents Morris's 'cubist' style of neo-Palladian villa, with an immediate precedent in Westcombe House, Blackheath, built for Lord Herbert in about 1729-30 (35b), and, further back in Morris's career, in one of his earliest works: Combe Bank, Kent, designed about 1725. Morris's cubist villa was his most original contribution to the neo-Palladian country house. He appears to have been attempting to break away from traditional country house models, developing a type of astylar villa that may owe something to the utilitarian style of the Office of Ordnance, whose Master General from 1725 was the 2nd Duke of Argyll, and where Morris succeeded to the post of Master Carpenter in 1734.

35. *Roger Morris (1695-1749)*
Whitton Place, Middlesex
Preliminary design for a villa
Elevation of the garden front
Insc. South Front toward the garden Letter A
Lit. & reprd. John Harris, *A Catalogue of British Drawings for
Architecture, Decoration... in American Collections*, 1971, p. 138
YALE CENTER FOR BRITISH ART, PAUL MELLON
COLLECTION

South Front toward the Garden Letter A

36. *William Hiorne (c. 1712-1776) & David Hiorne (died 1758)*
Gopsall Hall, Leicestershire
Design for the Dining Room
Plan with laid-back wall elevations with scale
*Insc. A Section of Dining Room Design'd for Charles Jennens Esqr.
with the Pannels plain, being to be Covered with Valuable Paintings
Signed W&D Hiorn*
Pen and wash (530 x 590)
RIBA Drawn as Collection

36a

The Hiornes' work at Gopsall, carried out between about 1750 and 1760, is characteristic of the activity of a provincial office, in this instance one established in Warwick. If anyone is laid under tribute it is Gibbs of the *Book of Architecture*, 1728, rather than Kent or Burlington of the *Designs of Inigo Jones...*, 1727. The doorways, the chimney-piece and the broken and fielded panels show no allegiance to neo-Palladianism, and are simply and sensibly Georgian. The proposed cove is richly ornamented with asymmetrical Rococo plasterwork, and Rococo too is the mirror-frame on the window wall. Although described as a dining-room, the location on the entry axis is that of a hall or saloon.

Generally, decoration emanating from a London man is more architectonic: the architect is in control. A provincial practice such as the Hiornes' placed more reliance upon the craftsman (such as the carver and the plasterer) to achieve a decorative effect. In particular, the Rococo was well received in the provinces, and the habit there of borrowing from printed pattern books often led to extreme examples of a style. The design for the Gopsall dining-room chimney-piece (*36b*) was made concurrently with James Paine's more classicising designs, (37) and could equally well have served for the 'best' dining-room (*37a*) that boasts a mirror likewise showing the influence of Chippendale's *Director* of 1754. *36a* shows the Library at Gopsall photographed just before the Hitler War.

36b

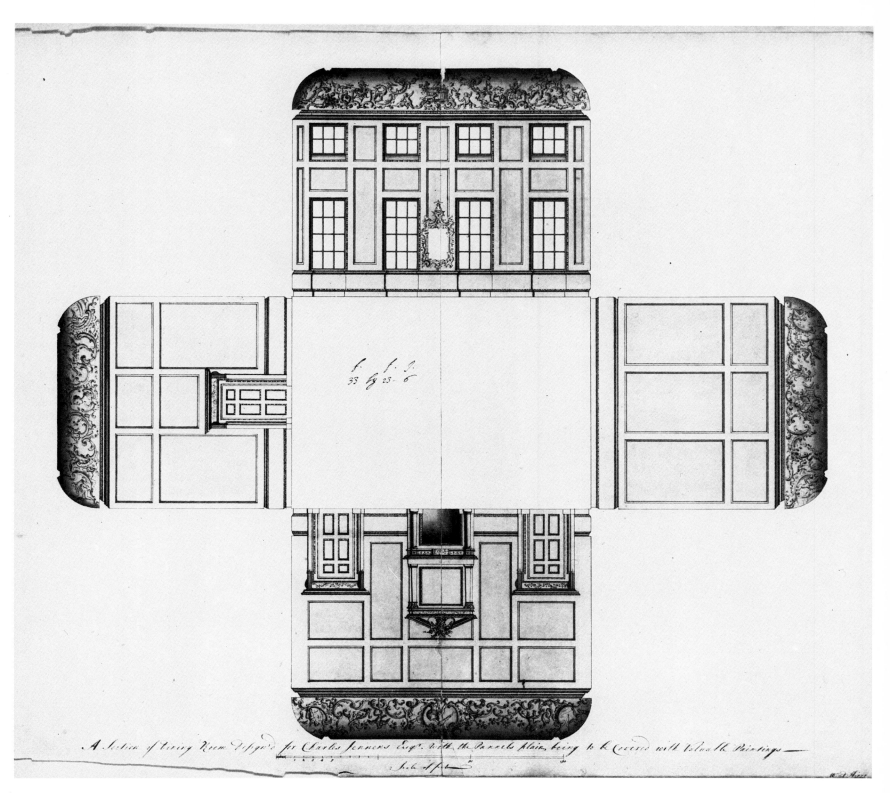

A Section of Living Room Design'd for Charles Jenners Esqr. with the Pannels plain, being to be Covered with Valuable Paintings —

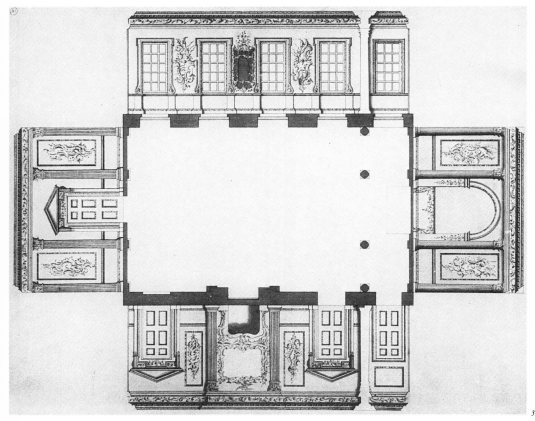

Gopsall Hall had been begun in about 1750 for Charles Jennens by a carpenter and joiner, John Westley, and completed by William and David Hiorne of Warwick. Theirs was the particularly sumptuous Rococo plaster decoration, which remained intact until the house was demolished in 1951.

Although Paine built a temple at Gopsall dedicated to Edward Holdsworth, the Virgil scholar, with its statue of *Religion* by Roubiliac, in the 1760s, his design (37) for the *Best Dining Room* was not executed. Although there are episodes in this decorative scheme that could be described as Rococo, notably the alternative manner of combining busts and ovals on the window wall, the chimney-piece and the double ovals framed by swags are reminders that this was the period of Sir William Chambers's and Robert Adam's Neoclassicism. *37a* is what may be an alternative design by the Hiornes' for the best dining room. It demonstrates the contrast between a sophisticated London master and a provincial. The Hiornes' habit of mixing Rococo and Classical elements in decoration shows how they fail the test of a sophisticated architecture, as they do also in the matter of how the room is proportioned and the relationship of one part to another.

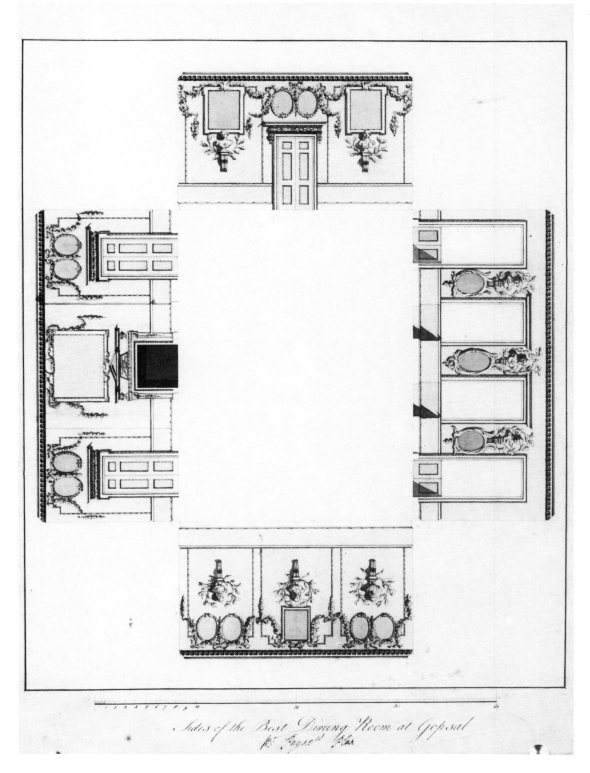

37. James Paine (1717-1789)
Gopsall Hall, Leicestershire
Design for the decoration of the Best Dining
Room with walls laid back, with scale
Insc. by Paine, *Sides of the Best Dining Room
at Gopsal* and in another hand, *Mr Payne's Plan*
Pen and coloured washes (510 x 355)
Lit. & reprd. Jill Lever, ed., *RIBA
Catalogue...O-R*, 1976, p. 12
RIBA DRAWINGS COLLECTION

38. John Sanderson (died 1774)
Kimberley Hall, Norfolk
Design for the Great Room
Plan of ceiling with laid-back wall elevations, with scale *Insc.*
A Design for the Great Room at Kimberly in Norfolk
Signed & dated. Sanderson 1770
Pen and watercolour (520 x 540)
Lit. & reprd. Jill Lever, *Architects' Designs for Furniture*, 1982,
p. 44, pl. II
RIBA DRAWINGS COLLECTION

This drawing comes from the Kimberley Park album. From about 1755 Sir Armine Wodehouse was employing Sanderson as contractor to enlarge the house, adding towers at the angles, to designs by Thomas Prowse, a gentleman-amateur architect. Sanderson also made proposals for the interior, and seems to have continued to provide designs over the next fifteen years, many of which were either not executed, or, if they were, have been destroyed. It is astonishing that even in 1770 Sanderson could offer alternative styles. Each bay or section provides a choice between Rococo and Neoclassical, although the ceiling is in a Chambersian style. The design for the chimney-piece is a curious marrying of funeral sculpture and a secular surround (*38a*). It was intended to commemorate John Wodehouse, one of the victors at the Battle of Agincourt. Victory and Fame hold a crown of laurels over his bas-relief portrait. This type of commemoration is common on tombs but rare on chimney-pieces.

38a

a Designe for the chimny piece in the Great Room at Kimberly

Sanderson 1770   A Design for the Great Room at Kimberley in Norfolk

THE NEO-PALLADIAN HOUSE   151

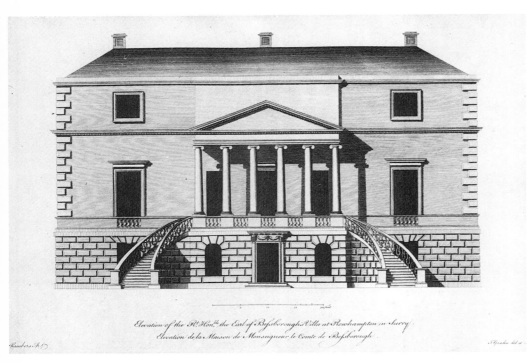

Elevation of the Rt. Honble. the Earl of Bessborough's Villa at Rowhampton in Surry.
Elevation de la Maison de Monseigneur le Comte de Bessborough.

39a

This unexecuted design (*39*) was made for John Lewis of Llanaeron. It represents a crucial stage in the evolution of Chambers's villas. In 1760 he built Roehampton, Surrey, for Lord Bessborough (*39a* shows the garden front, in the engraving from John Woolfe and James Gandon, *Vitruvius Britannicus*, VI, 1767) and in 1763 Duddingstone, Midlothian, for Lord Abercorn (*39b*). Llanaeron stands midway between these, where the portico achieves the effect of a temple feature, standing upon the ground with a low stylobate or base of six steps. At Duddingstone, the portico rests upon a base of three steps, accentuating the temple look. All three designs are Neoclassical reinterpretations of the neo-Palladian villas of Colen Campbell and more recently of Isaac Ware. Llanaeron is Campbell's Stourhead, with the order changed to Ionic.

39b

THE NEOCLASSICAL HOUSE

39. *Sir William Chambers (1723-1796)*
Llanaeron, Cardiganshire
Design for a villa
Elevation of entrance or portico front
Insc. Front Elevation and in another hand, *Llanerchaern*
Pen and watercolour (365 x 590)
Lit. & reprd. John Harris, *Sir William Chambers*, 1970,
pp 46-7, 215, pl. 61
B.S.J. Pardoe Collection

40a

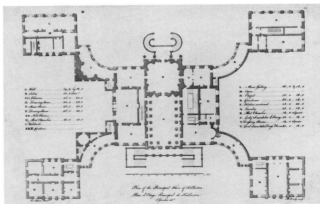

40b

Kedleston is a case of architects' musical chairs. Matthew Bret-tingham was first consulted by Sir Nathaniel Curzon *c*.1758, proposed one of his big neo-Palladian houses with two out-riding pavilions, and actually got as far as to build the north-east one. Then he was superceded by James Paine almost within the year. In fact it is Paine who introduced the novelty of the huge columnar and basilica-like hall. Paine exhibited his design in 1759. Then James Stuart seems to have been consulted for interior works; and not more than another year had passed before Paine was himself superceded by Adam, although both seem to have worked amicably together for some while. Both Paine and Adam observed the weakness of the south front but whereas Paine proposed a huge semi-circular portico-collonade, Adam made the centre into a triumphal arch married to a Pantheon-like rotonda. It had been Adam's intention to repeat on the south the existing north-east and north-west pavilions linked to the angles of the north front by quadrant collonades, with his own pavilions seen at the top of the plan in *40b*, one housing a Music Room, the other a Greenhouse and Chapel. These would have been in his neo-Palladian or neo-Burlington style, but were never built. They were proposed at the end of building operations on the south front, and must immediately follow the reduced project as here exhibited. Here the pavilions to the end of the front are similarly neo-Burlingtonian and incorporate some of the elements that Adam had been using in his modifications of John Carr's Harewood House, Yorkshire, at about the same time.

40. Robert Adam (1728–1792)
Kedleston Hall, Derbyshire
Design for the south front
Elevation, with scale
Insc. South Front of Kedleston House with the new additions and
Extends 182 feet
Signed & dated. Robt Adam Archt 1765
Pen and watercolour
TRUSTEES OF THE KEDLESTON ESTATE TRUSTS

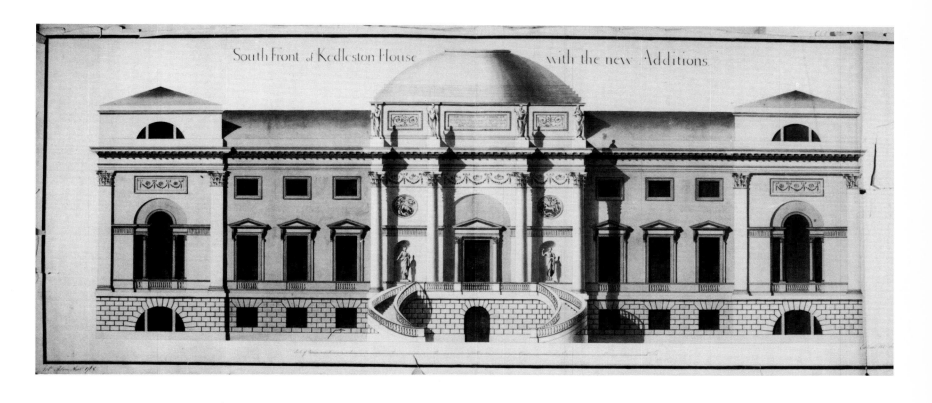

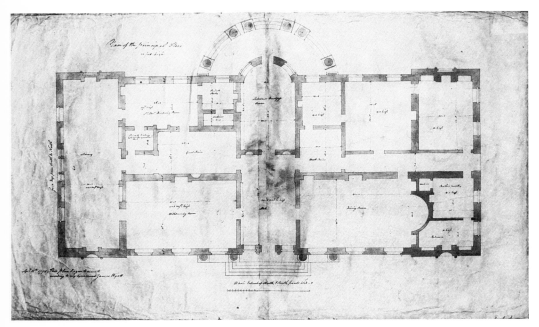

41a

James Wyatt signed an agreement with Sir Thomas Acland on 15 April 1775 for a new house: *41a*, Wyatt's plan of the ground floor for Killerton, is inscribed by him *April 14th 1775 This Plan I agree to execute according to my Agreement James Wyatt*. For reasons that are not yet apparent, but probably as the result of a row induced by the claret-swilling architect, Acland rejected the project, and had a smaller house designed in 1778 by John Johnson.

By 1775 Wyatt had already become the alternative to Robert Adam. Wyatt's brand of Neoclassicism, particularly in interiors, was often more palatable because it was simpler and less fussy. On the whole Wyatt catered for the average rather than the exceptional client. Nonetheless there is great distinction in this Killerton elevation, with its wings demarcated by pilasters and centred by aedicules, its decorative bas-reliefs (probably to have been in Coadestone) above the windows, the handsome tripartite entrance set under a shallow relieving arch, and above this ovals draped with Gallic festoons. There are hints in this design of the Roman severity that Wyatt would adopt for his finest country house, Dodington Park, Gloucestershire, in 1798.

As far as is known Wyatt was his own colourist, although in 1794 Joseph Farington had described John Dixon as 'the artist who is employed by Wyatt to draw for him'.

41. James Wyatt (1746-1813)
Killerton Park, Devon
Design for a new house
Elevation of entrance front
Watercolour (520 x 700)
RIBA Drawings Collection

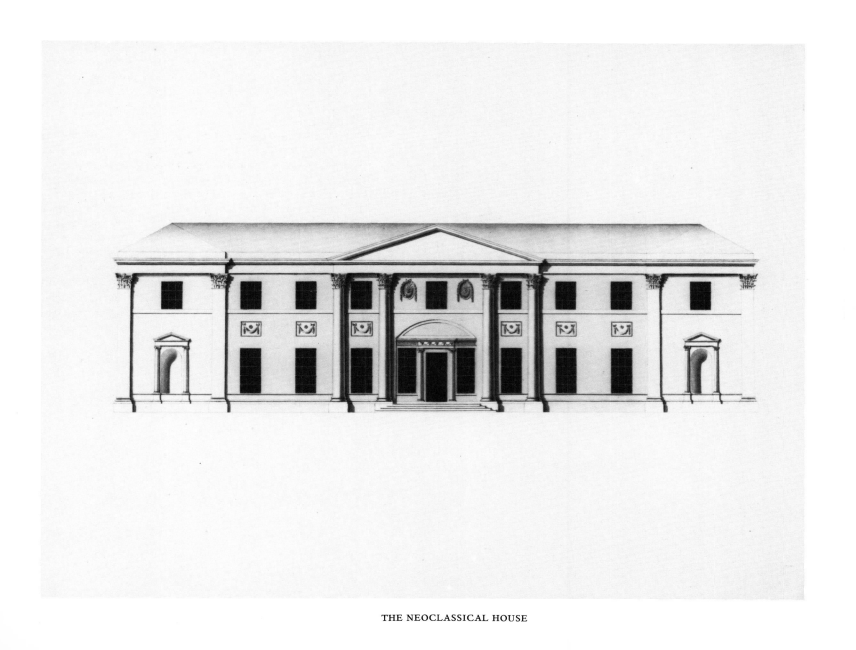

THE NEOCLASSICAL HOUSE

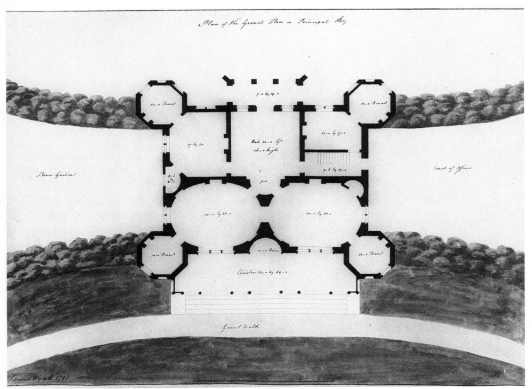

42b

In 1791 Wyatt was engaged upon two commissions of similar size, one of which, Broke Hall, Suffolk, built for Philip Broke, was in the Gothic style. However the quality of this watercolour is so outstanding as to imply a special commmission, and the designs may well have been offered to Queen Charlotte for Frogmore House, near Windsor Castle. Although Wyatt rebuilt Frogmore in Classical style around an earlier 17th-century house after 1792, it is known that he had made alternative designs the previous year; *42a* is the elevation of the garden front of the 1791 design. These could have been rejected for a compromise solution, in a style more suited to the Queen's taste: James Wyatt's signed and dated 1791 plan of the ground floor (*42b*) is an extremely felicitous arrangement of octagons, ovals and semi-circular shapes and niches, clearly intended to be classical in treatment.

After beginning to practice in about 1768, Wyatt only gradually turned to Gothick . His only Gothick house before Mrs Montagu's Sandleford Priory of about 1780 is Sheffield Place, Sussex, begun in 1776. It was not until he had digested his experiences at Windsor Castle, after 1796, and the many cathedral restorations, after 1786, that Wyatt began to design in a more convincing picturesque way.

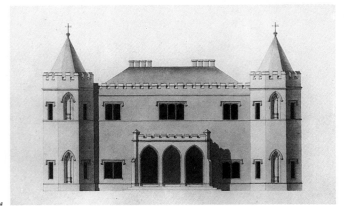

42a

THE NEOCLASSICAL HOUSE

42. *James Wyatt (1746-1813)*
Frogmore House, Berkshire
Unexecuted design for a new Royal Lodge
Elevation, with scale
Signed & dated. James Wyatt 1791
Watercolour (459 x 604)
YALE CENTER FOR BRITISH ART, PAUL MELLON
COLLECTION

James Wyatt 1791

Although this design is not inscribed, it belongs in both style and technique to those made for Kedleston, Derbyshire, for Sir Nathaniel Curzon in about 1757. Among related designs are at least two for Earl Spencer's Wimbledon House, decorated by Stuart at about the same time. When Horace Walpole visited Wimbledon in about 1758, he remarked upon 'a closet, ornamented and painted by Mr Stewart, the ornaments in a good antique taste. A Hymen, the Allegro & Penseroso, on the ceiling and in compartments, villianously painted'. ('Visits to Country Seats', *Walpole Society*, XVI, 15: *43a*, Stuart's design for a room at Wimbledon is possibly for the closet seen by Walpole.) Stuart had anticipated Robert Adam in conceiv‑ing a room as an entity, to be presented to the client complete with recommendations for the placing of furniture and pictures. William Kent had been one of the first professional English architects to make such all‑embracing designs, but his innova‑tions in the 1720s seem never to have attracted attention. The exhibited design is probably for the Great Dining Room. The chimney‑piece is almost identical to that proposed for Sir Nathaniel Curzon's Great Saloon at Kedleston.

43. James Stuart (1713-1788)
Wimbledon House, Surrey
Design for the decoration and furnishings of a room
Pen, pencil and watercolour (180 x 290)
Lit. & reprd. John Harris, 'Newly Acquired Designs by James
Stuart in the British Architectural Library, Drawings Collec-
tion', *Architectural History*, v. 22, 1979, pp. 74-5, pl. 18, & Jill
Lever, *Architects' Designs for Furniture*, 1982, pp 46-7, pls 13a,
13b, and pl. III
RIBA Drawings Collection

44. Sir William Chambers (1723-1796)
Buckingham House, St James's Park, London
Design for the ceiling of the Second Drawing Room
Insc. on verso, by Chambers *Casts/Cipriani for painting 17 pictures & 4 Genii Ls 225/Catton for painting in Gold & Colours all/the Ornaments and the four Angles & mould. ls 120/Norman fr. pasting up the Work 12. 12/ Ls 357. 12*
Watercolour (460 x 355)
Lit. & reprd. John Harris, *Sir William Chambers,* 1970, pp 217-18, pl. 119
RIBA DRAWINGS COLLECTION

Buckingham House was the predecessor of Buckingham Palace; in 1762 it was purchased for Queen Charlotte, and hence afterwards was known as The Queen's House. The alterations and internal decorations were in the charge of Chambers, for whom Giovanni Battista Cipriani prepared or coloured this design. In this particular case the inscription reveals that Cipriani provided the inset decorative paintings, Charles Catton the ornamental work, and Samuel Norman, a gilder, pasted the work up into the ceiling proper. *44a* shows the Second Drawing Room as recorded by W.H. Pyne in his *History of the Royal Residences,* 1818.

Cipriani was acting as a professional colourist to Chambers, as he had acted in a similar capacity to other architects, including Robert Adam. However, he was mostly Chambers's man, and throughout the 1760s Chambers's designs were to be made more attractive to the client through Cipriani's artistic skills. This is an early example of an architectural design deliberately made into an object of aesthetic merit. Very soon afterwards Adam would follow suit, outbidding Chambers in the employment of colourists.

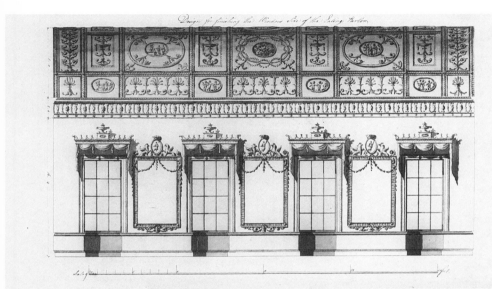

45a

45b

Headfort House was begun in 1760, when the owner was Sir Thomas Taylor; but by 1766 he had become the Earl of Bective, and so, as a nobleman in society, required something more sophisticated than a plain house designed by Irish builders. In 1765 he had toyed with designs by Sir William Chambers, but it was not until 1771 that Robert Adam began the slow transformation of the interiors of a more or less undecorated house. Even after this date various designs were rejected. (45a-b show Robert Adam's designs for the end and window wall of the 'Eating Parlour', also dated 1771). The Hall was decorated in 1771, and the Saloon in 1772; but the Dining Room or Eating Parlour, not until after designs had been made in 1773. Therefore, these late designs form the link between Headfort House and Derby House or Home House, London, both of 1773, and representative of the high-water mark of Adam's filigree style, created expressly to provide an all-embracing ornamental cosmetic to a room. This drawing is an admirable example of Adam's use of professional colourists, in this case George Richardson, who described himself in 1774 as 'draughtsman and designer' to the Adam brothers, for 'upwards of eighteen years'.

45. Robert Adam (1728-1792)
Headfort House, Co. Meath, Ireland
Design for the Dining-Room
Section showing chimney wall and cove of ceiling, with scale
Insc. by Adam, *Design for finishing the Chimney side of the Eating Parlour.*
For The Right Honble The Earl of Bective
Signed & dated. Robert Adam archt. 1771
Pen and watercolour (460 x 620)
Lit. & reprd. John Harris, *Headfort House and Robert Adam,* 1973, pls 27-8
YALE CENTER FOR BRITISH ART, PAUL MELLON COLLECTION

Drawn by J.F. Neale.
Engraved by W. Wallis

MILTON ABBAS.
DORSETSHIRE.

46a

Lord Milton, 'an unmannerly imperios Lord who has treated me as he does every body ill,' as Sir William Chambers bemoaned in 1773, had been employing John Vardy for work at the old Abbey house. Following Vardy's death in 1765 Chambers was summoned to the substantial task of finishing the house, between 1769 and 1775. The entrance front, for example, seen in *46a* drawn by J.F. Neale in the early 19th century, although built by Chambers, must surely incorporate a design by Vardy, for it is but a child of Kent's Esher. Once Chambers could no longer stand the arrogant, over-bearing Lord, Milton then turned to James Wyatt. Wyatt's decoration of the Gallery in 1776 was thus an internal facing to a room basically by Chambers, whose windows these are. Wyatt's style follows the prevailing Adamesque idiom of delicate, shallow mouldings, lacking any strong articulation or shadow. Chambers would have done it differently, with a ceiling more Roman in style and with clearer separation of the compartments. Wyatt's curtains and pelmets demonstrate the perennial problem of adapting curtains to Gothic windows.

46. *James Wyatt (1741-1813)*
Milton Abbey, Dorset
Design for the decoration of the Gallery
Elevation of window wall, with scale
Insc. by Wyatt, *Window Side of the Gallery Milton Abbey*
Signed & dated. Jas. Wyatt July 1776
Pen and coloured washes (350 x 520)
Lit. & reprd. RIBA Drawings Collection, Catalogue... Wyatt ed.
Derek Linstrum, 1973
RIBA Drawings Collection

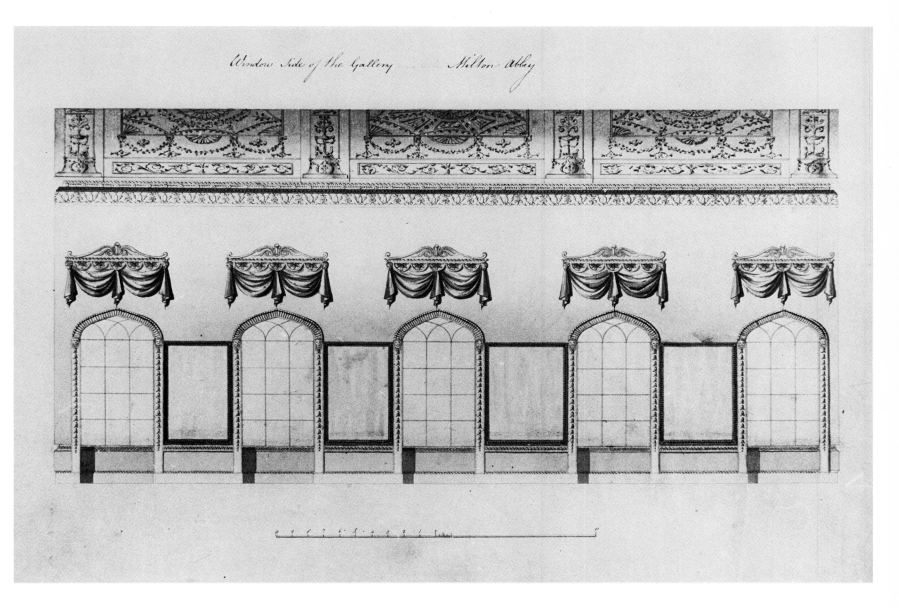

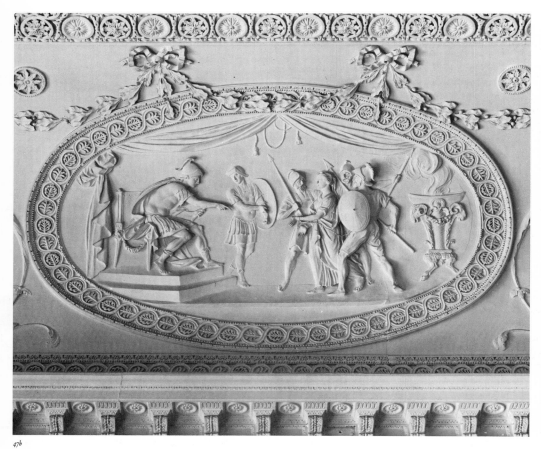

47b

47a

Sandbeck was remodelled for the 4th Earl of Scarborough from about 1763. The Great Room is a huge chamber set transversely across the first floor front of the house, not unlike an Elizabethan Great or High Chamber. As a room (47a), it is one of Paine's noblest compositions, in style a little severe and Roman in contrast to the more feminine, shallow ornamental style of Robert Adam. The excellent plasterwork (47b) was executed by Thomas Collins. Paine's career was extraordinary in that it embraced neo-Palladianism and Neoclassicism, for not only was Paine the most successful follower of William Kent, but he survived to die only three years before Adam.

47. *James Paine (1717-1789)*
Sandbeck Park, Yorkshire
Design for the ceiling of the Great Room
Plan of centre with elevation of long cove and half elevation
of short side, with scale
*Insc. Finishing Design'd for the Cieling and Cove to the Great Room
at Sandbeck*
Pen and watercolour (350 x 475)
Lit. M. Girouard, 'Sandbeck Park', *Country Life*,
CXXXVIII, 1965, pp 966-7
RIBA DRAWINGS COLLECTION

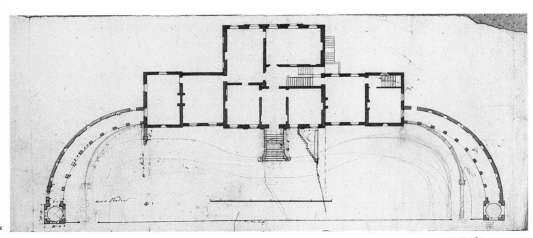

48a

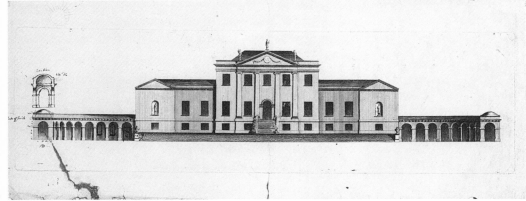

48b

Anthony Bacon required a modest surburban villa on the edge of London, and for this in 1768 Newton first provided a house with dining-room, drawing-room, common parlour and common eating room on the main floor, but with a fairly grand staircase. Typically for the eighteenth century the kitchens were placed in one of the wings, necessitating bringing food through the 'arched passage' or quadrant and up the smaller, servants' staircase to the dining-room.

For some reason this design was abandoned and Newton produced a much larger house, really a proper villa with wings of five bays, with a pilastered frontispiece. His original plan has survived, but the elevation is only known from an engraving specially made by Newton (48a-b), which includes the plan and shows the main body of the house as built from 1768, but with the addition of quadrant arcades, shown in lighter hatching, perhaps not built, or proposed after the completion of the house.

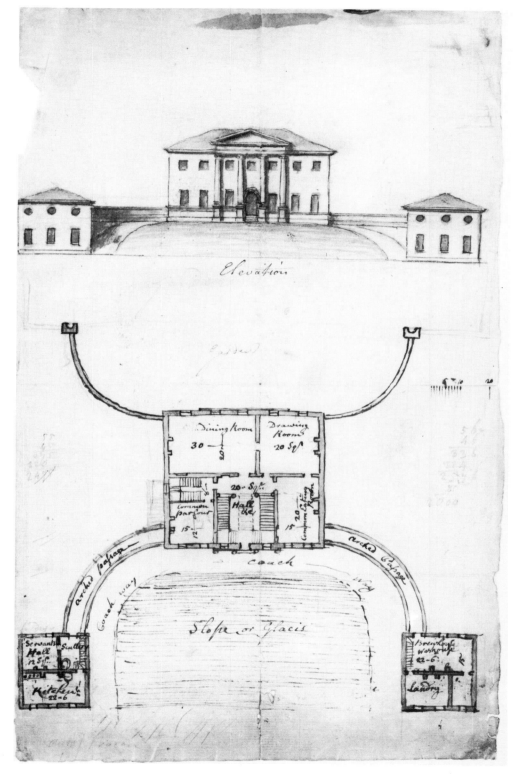

48. *William Newton (1735-1790)*
Highams, Walthamstow, Essex
Preliminary design for Anthony Bacon's house
Plan, and elevation of court front in perspective, with scale
Insc. Anthony Bacon
Pencil, pen and wash (335 x 210)
Lit. & reprd. John Harris, *Georgian Country Houses*, 1968, pl. 28
RIBA DRAWINGS COLLECTION

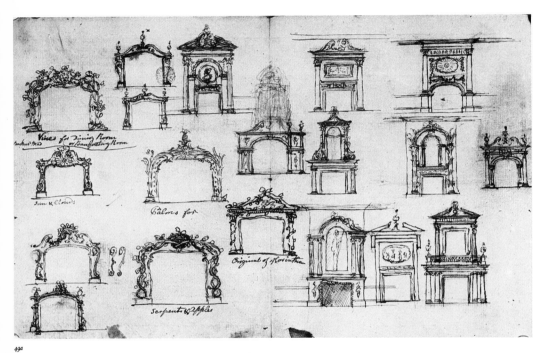

49a

Newton was an unconventional architect. Although the exteriors of Highams were not, in fact, exceptional, many of his designs are quirky, as if he was purposely trying to be different. This is especially so with his interiors. He is addicted to ornament, in this case carved in wood, or as 'stuco', mixing Rococo and Neoclassical motifs. This design may not have been excuted, but the room fits one shown on the engraved plan (*48a*).

Newton's strong idiosyncracy in achieving a personal interior effect is no better demonstrated that in some of his sheets of studies for chimney-pieces (*49a*). He endowed the chimney-piece with far more importance and character than perhaps any of his contemporaries, Chambers, Adam and Wyatt not excepted.

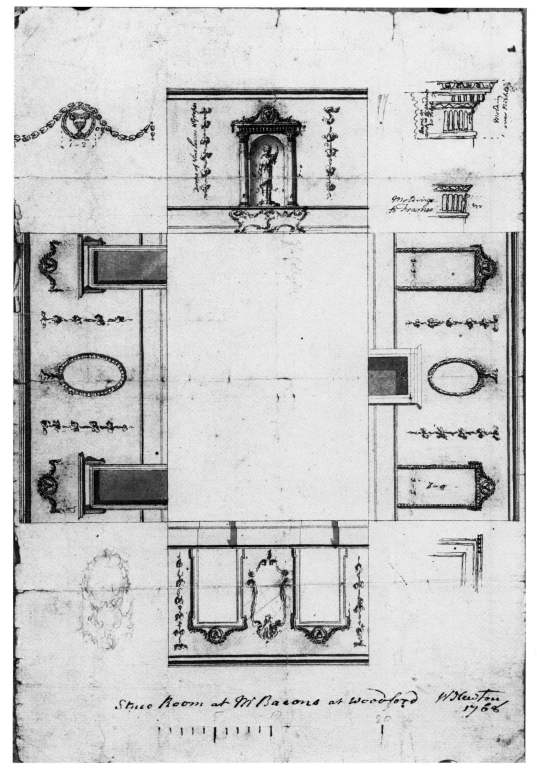

49. *William Newton (1735-1790)*
Highams, Walthamstow, Essex
Design for the 'Stuco' Room
Plan with laid-back wall elevations, with
details of mouldings and ornament
Insc. Stuco Room at Mr Bacons at Woodford
W Newton 1768
Pen, pencil and wash (310 x 200)
RIBA DRAWINGS COLLECTION

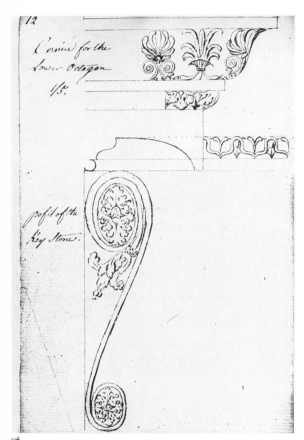

50b

50a

It does not matter that Carlton House is not a country house proper, for this section is an excellent representation of the French-enriched Neoclassical style that Holland introduced to England. Encouraged by the Gallic sympathies of his patron's Whig coterie he remodelled Carlton House for the Prince of Wales between 1783 and 1796, employing the French entrepreneur Dominique Daguerre for furnishings. Even if not so admitted by himself, Holland was an admirer of Sir William Chambers's interiors at Somerset House, where a proper French Neoclassical style had been achieved from 1776. The hall, tribune (or octagon) and staircase in this section demonstrate this admiration. One of Holland's record drawings (50b) from the Carlton House sketchbook shows the 'Cornice for the Lower Octagon' and 'profil of the Key stone'; the Octagon is the left-hand compartment in Holland's design section. As furnished, there were minor differences in the decoration, seen for example in the illustration of the vestibule or hall from Pyne's *Royal Residences*, 1818 (50a).

Because Carlton House was demolished in 1827-8, the best surviving memorial to Holland's style is now Southill House, Bedfordshire, which he designed for Samuel Whitbread from 1796.

THE NEOCLASSICAL HOUSE

50. Henry Holland (1745-1806)
Carlton House, Pall Mall, London
Design for the interior
North-south section through portico & first hall, hall, octagon
& staircase, and first ante-room
Insc. Carlton House, section through the Portico, Hall & Tribune
Pen and watercolour (355 x 716)
Lit. Dorothy Stroud, *Henry Holland*, 1976, chapters 6 & 7; H.M.
Colvin (ed), *The History of the King's Works*, VI, 1973
YALE CENTER FOR BRITISH ART, PAUL MELLON COLLECTION

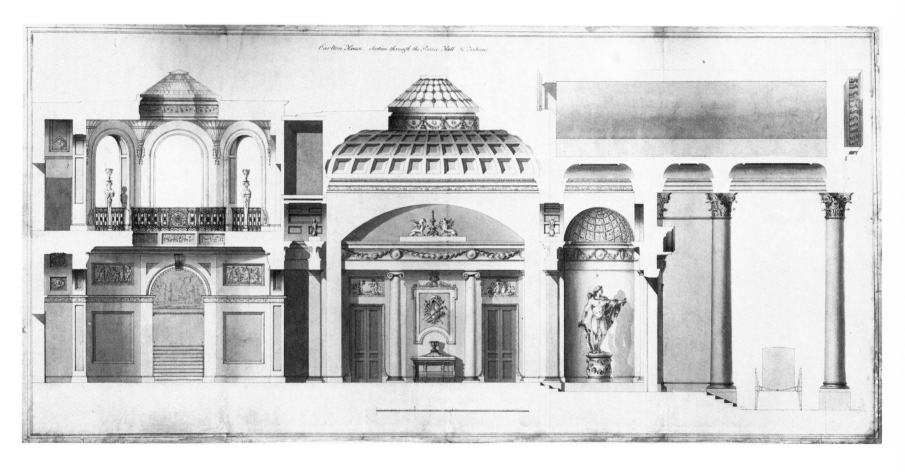

THE NEOCLASSICAL HOUSE

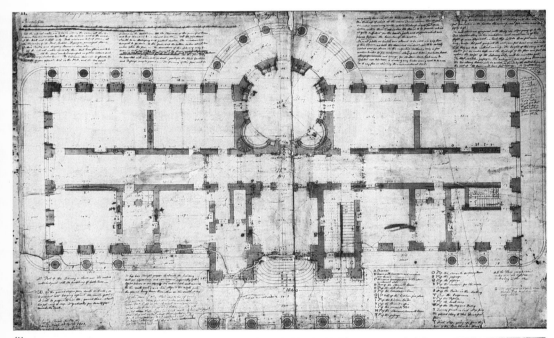

51a

51b

Rosneath was built for the 5th Duke of Argyll, from 1803 to 1806, on a superb site on the Firth of Clyde. It was one of the few houses in Britain that could stand beside any built by C.H. Ledoux. Indeed it would not be surprising if Bonomi had seen Ledoux's work at first hand or had access to the engravings of *L'Architecture considérée* before its publication in 1804. There are echoes, too, in Rosneath of the work of Friedrich Gilly whom Bonomi had probably met in London in 1797-98.

This front of Rosneath should also be compared to the Duke of Shrewsbury's Heythrop House, Oxfordshire, where there is an uncanny similarity, both in the use of a triple order and in the long, low bulk of the house. Bonomi may well have been involved in the finishings of Heythrop's interior, work that appears to have dragged on through the century. It should not surprise us that Bonomi was receptive to European influences, for he was born in Rome, educated at the Collegio Romano, and studied under the Marchese Teodoli, before he came to London to work for Robert and James Adam in 1767. Rosneath was built to stand free of any encumbrances, and to this end the offices were placed underground, approached by a tunnel. The portico was a proper *porte-cochère*, marked as such by its central column, which was echoed by that of the trio marking the ends of the front. 51a, the plan of the ground floor, is a working drawing, fully annotated with comments and instructions by Bonomi and dated March and April 1803: he describes Rosneath as in 'North Britain'. 51b is a section of Rosneath from north to south, also from a set of working drawings, in this case showing the positioning of chimney flues. It is dated July 1803 and addressed from 76 Great Titchfield Street, London.

This noble house was gutted by fire in 1947 when derequisitioned after the war, and was finally blown up in 1961.

51. Joseph Bonomi (1739-1808)
Rosneath, Dunbartonshire
Design for a new house
Perspective
Pen and watercolour (620 x 990)
Lit. & reprd. Jill Lever & Margaret Richardson, *The Art of the Architect*, 1984, 13, pl. 45
RIBA Drawings Collection

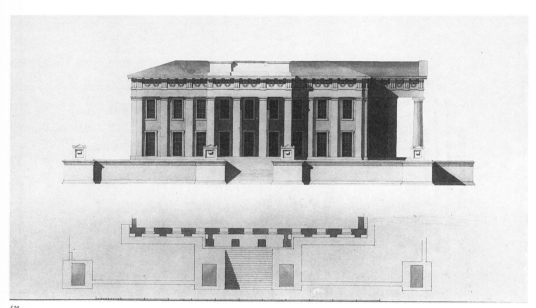

52a

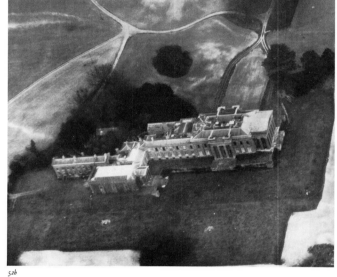

52b

The Grange was a distinguished seventeenth-century house by William Samwell. In 1805 Henry Drummond summoned Wilkins to remodel and encase it, and the near-completed house was commemorated by two designs exhibited at the Royal Academy in 1809. The house had always been dramatically sited, on the edge of a hill and overlooking a valley landscaped in the eighteenth century to provide a natural lake. Wilkins responded to the drama by transforming the old house into a striking Greek temple, using the fifth-century Greek Doric order. The terrace was marked out by plinths resembling ancient Sicilian tombs, and upon this Wilkins erected his temple, the portico based upon the Theseum, 'one of the noblest remains of ancient magnificence' as he described it in his *Atheniensia* in 1816. In *52a*, his design for the side of the Grange, the plan of the wall marks that of the seventeenth-century house, which he simply encased in a neo-Greek skin based upon the Choragic Monument to Thrasyllus.

When C.R. Cockerell went there in January 1823 he enthused 'nothing can be finer... more classical or like the finest Poussino... its elevation on terraces gives it that which is essential to the effect of Grecian architecture & which no modern imitations possess'. Indeed no other country house in Britain quite captivates the Greek spirit of site and place as does the Grange, seen from the air in *52b*.

52. *William Wilkins (1778-1839)*
The Grange, Hampshire
Design for the east or portico front
Elevation in perspective
Pen and wash (330 x 585)
Lit. & reprd. R.W. Liscombe, *William Wilkins*, 1980, pp 59-61
RIBA DRAWINGS COLLECTION

53b

53a

Soane was particularly affected by the experience of designing Tyringham, built for the banker William Mackworth Praed from 1793; in his *Memoirs* he writes that 'this villa, with its numerous offices, and the lodge, were completed and occupied in the year 1797, after having engaged a large portion of six of the most happy years of my life.' The design is a logical development from themes expressed in his *Sketches in Architecture* of 1793, amplifying the fertility of his imagination and extending its play and concern with spatial invention. Indeed, this banker's house was progressing concurrently with Soane's work on the Bank of England, and there are distinct parallels between the treatment of the Bank's Lothbury front and Tyringham's rather francophile elevations. In this house Soane was trying to reach out for a style that owed little to precedent, and was eventually to be fully achieved at Pellwell Hall, Staffordshire, in 1822. Tryingham is celebrated also for its gateway, a primitive, stripped Classical design, recognised as one of the great monuments of European Neoclassicism. The house (*53a*) was altered by G.F Rees in 1909, and the gardens (*53b*) were amplified by Lutyens in 1910 and 1926.

53. *Sir John Soane (1753-1837)*
Tyringham Hall, Buckinghamshire
Perspective view of house and service wing from south east,
drawn by J.M. Gandy (1771-1843)
Insc. (in pencil) *Tyringam, Bedfordshire, seat of W. Praed by Gandy*
Pen and ink with watercolour (573 x 905)
VICTORIA AND ALBERT MUSEUM

54a

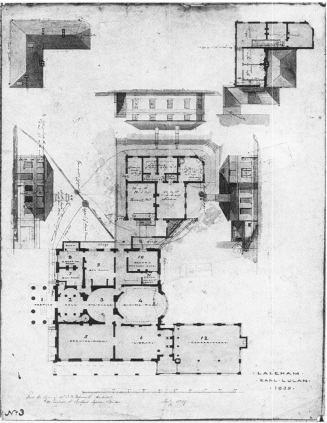

54b

Papworth can be considered as the Regency architect *par excellence*, whose work epitomises, more than any other's, the best of what the landed gentry and lesser nobility required for accomodation. Laleham is typical of one family's patronage of their favoured architect over a number of years. In 1802 the old manor house was bought by the 2nd Earl of Lucan (1764‑1839), following their abandonment of Castlebar House, Ireland, burnt down in the troubles of 1798. The house then built by Papworth was a simple, chaste block with a single story Doric portico, all very unassuming and characteristic of the average in Regency house design. In 1839 Papworth was again summoned by Lord Lucan, to add a verandah and, of course, a conservatory, and to enrich the exterior with ornamental details such as the Greek key‑pattern frieze and recessed panels. If the upper story of the portico was also added at this time, it has since been demolished. Basically, Papworth's adornments in the 1830s were of an ornamental nature, enriching an otherwise plain house. *54a*, a perspective prepared by Papworth, slightly ante‑dates the 1839 elevation, while the plan of the house, made in July 1839 (*54b*), was principally to show the addition of offices.

54. John Buonarotti Papworth (1775-1847)
Laleham House, Middlesex
Design for alterations and additions
Elevation of entrance front, with scale
Insc. The Seat of Earl Lucan Laleham 1839
Pen, pencil and wash (430 x 610)
Lit. RIBA Catalogue...Papworth , ed. George McHardy, 1977,
pp 88-90
RIBA Drawings Collection

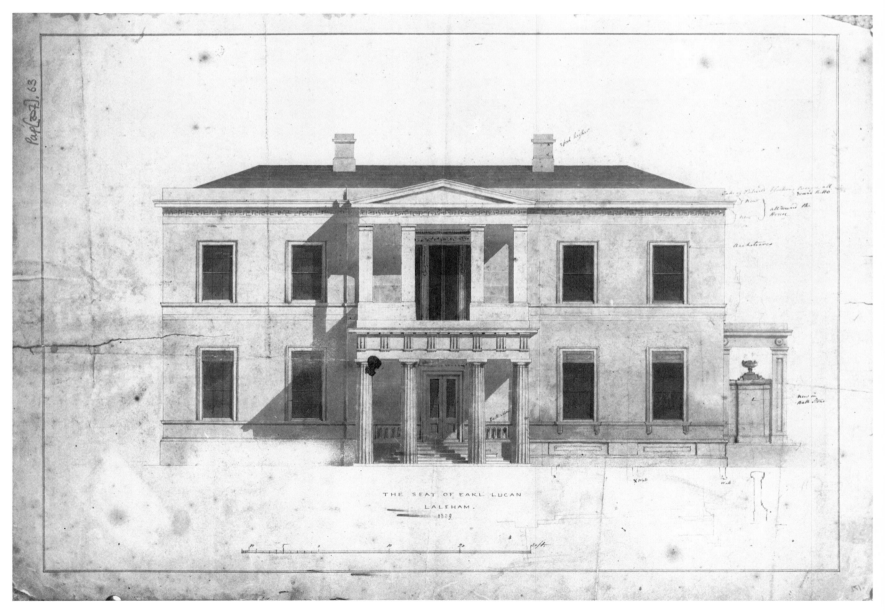

THE SEAT OF EARL LUCAN
LALEHAM.
1839

55. *John Buonarotti Papworth (1775-1847)*
Little Grove, East Barnet, Hertfordshire
Design for the decoration and furnishings of the Dining-Room
Laid-out wall elevations, with scale
Signed & dated. J.B. Papworth Archt 1839
Lit. & reprd. RIBA Catalogue... Papworth, ed. George McHardy,
1977, pp 119-23, pl. 31; Jill Lever, *Architects' Designs for
Furniture*, 1982, pp 64-6, pl. 31
RIBA DRAWINGS COLLECTION

55a

In 1827 Little Grove had been purchased by Frederick Cass, the son of William Cass, a merchant in the City of London. Papworth had probably been involved with Cass's nearby house at Beaulieu Lodge, Winchmore Hill. At Little Grove he substantially re-decorated the interior at various times, in 1828-33, 1836, 1839, 1843 and in 1849, a year before Papworth died. The folder of designs for Little Grove demonstrates Papworth's extraordinary versatility, for he was able to provide elegant rooms, vermin grates for drains, closets for the childrens' clogs, or Gardenesque flower beds. For the new dining-room Papworth has provided a characteristic interior in what might have been described as the 'Modern Grecian Taste', the motifs and ornament in a Regency style, but by this date already becoming coarser and more eclectic. The drawing shows Papworth's complete control of every detail, in a tradition that goes back to James Stuart, William Chambers and Robert Adam. Another detail, (55a) of one wall from a design for a drawing-room for James Morrison, demonstrates Papworth's meticulous attention to the placing of furniture. It was made in 1831-32. Exactly a century later, Little Grove was demolished.

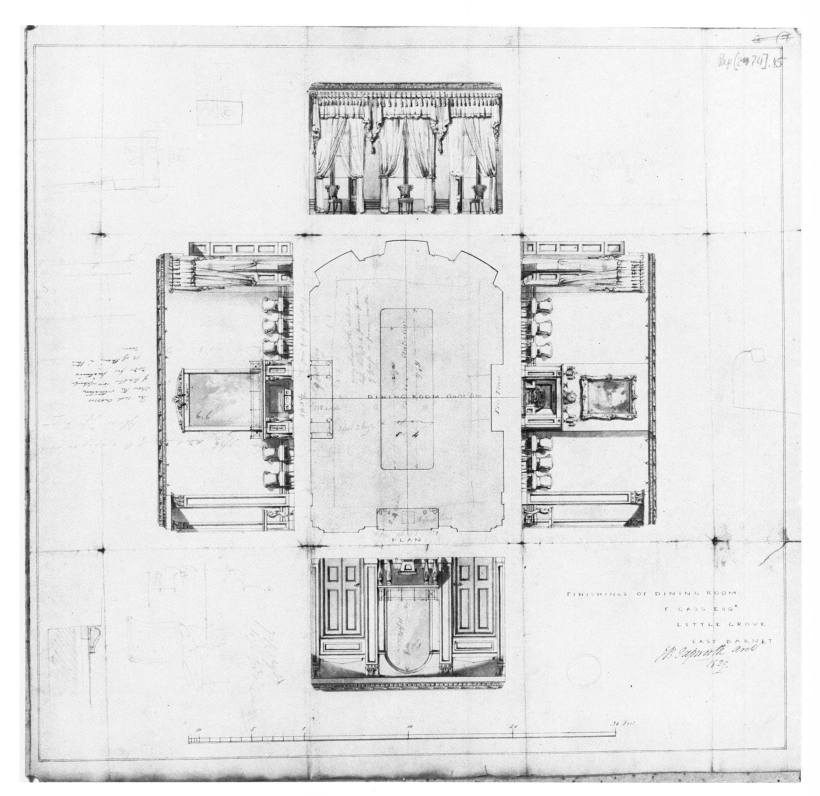

FINISHINGS OF DINING ROOM
F. CASS ESQ.
LITTLE GROVE
EAST BARNET

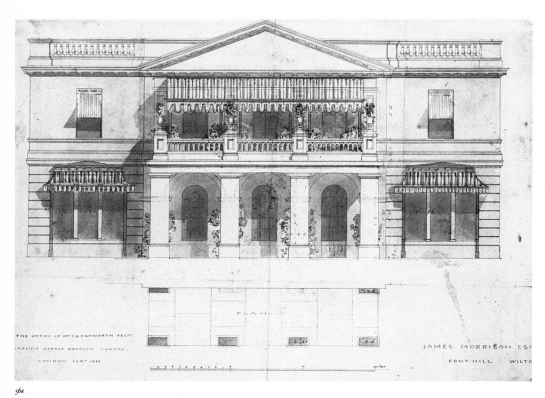

56a

The great classical house at Fonthill, known as 'Fonthill Splendens', was demolished in 1807 when William Beckford finally moved into Fonthill Abbey. One Palladian pavilion survived, and eventually this was bought in 1829 by James Morrison, and charmingly converted into a tiny Regency villa by Papworth. The Boudoir design is a remarkable document for the architect has appended to it his recommendations for the distemper colours to be used. It is perhaps worth recalling that R. Ackermann in his *Repository of the Arts* was also offering distemper and fabric colours at about the same time, a venture in which Papworth had some interest. *56a* is Papworth's design for adding a Regency porch to the Palladian pavilion of old Fonthill Splendens.

56. *John Buonarotti Papworth (1775-1847)*
Fonthill, Wiltshire
Design for decorating the Boudoir
Plan of ceiling with laid-back wall elevations, with scale
Pen and coloured washes and coloured distemper (330 x 460)
Lit. RIBA Catalogue... Papworth, ed. George McHardy, 1977,
pp 115-16
RIBA DRAWINGS COLLECTION

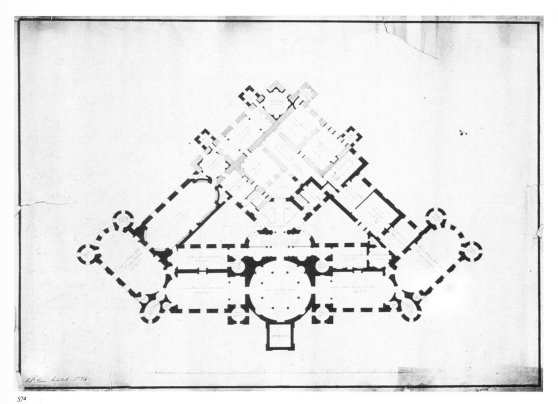

57a

Robert Adam's proposed additions to Barnbougle Castle are dated 1774, and were for a client—Neil Primrose, 3rd Earl of Rosebery—who was his contemporary. It is very difficult to know just how serious this astonishing project was, and whether it ever really was anticipated to lead to a building programme; there has always been a tradition that Lord Rosebery dreamed up the project only to impress Mary Vincent, whom he was courting as his second wife. Certainly all is on a scale that out-bids Syon or Luton Hoo.

Barnbougle was an old Scottish castle, done up at various times since the sixteenth century. Adam retained it, using it as the apex of the triangle from which his curious V-shaped plan (57a) extended. Seen in perspective, Adam's design con-veys the impression of a vast, curtain-walled edifice, and he can-not have been unmindful of the effect of the larger Mediaeval castles. This was a period in his career when he was responsive to the tradition in Scotland for castellated architecture, and keen to provide a national idiom of his own. Adam could have seen triangular planning in Piedmont, but with Barnbougle it is the scale that impresses, and for sequences of rooms on this scale the nearest precedent is Vanbrugh's Blenheim: indeed that first of Picturesque architects would have revelled in this dream castle.

(Professor Alistair Rowan ed.)

57. *Robert Adam (1728-1792)*
Barnbougle, West Lothian, Scotland
Design for a castle-style house built around the old tower
Perspective of west front
Signed & dated. Robt Adam Architect 1774
Pen and watercolour (440 x 595)
Lit. & reprd. Alan Tait, 'Robert Adam's Picturesque Architec-
ture', *Burlington Magazine*, July 1981, pp 421-2, fig. 38; Alistair
Rowan, *Robert & James Adam : Designs for Castles and Country
Villas*, 1985
THE EARL OF ROSEBERY

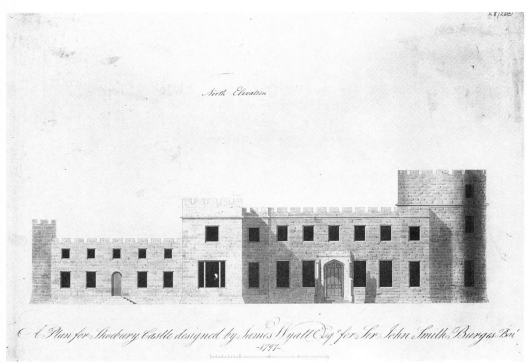

North Elevation

A Plan for Shoebury Castle designed by James Wyatt Esq for Sir John Smith Burges Bar.
-1797-

58a

In 1796, when Wyatt became Surveyor General of the Royal Works after Sir William Chamber's death, one of his responsibilities was to maintain Windsor Castle and its dependencies, the latter comprising the Queen's Lodge and the Lower Lodge (*58b*), built by Chambers in 1776 and 1779, in a plain, utilitarian castle style. Although not built, Shoebury is Wyatt's first experiment in a castle manner (*58a* shows the north front elevation). Norris Castle on the Isle of Wight followed in 1799, Pennsylvania Castle, Dorset in 1800, and Kew Palace in Surrey in 1801, concurrent with Wyatt's restorations at Windsor Castle. While it is not entirely certain if Wyatt saw this style as useful for situations by water, it seems uncanny that Shoebury, Norris and Pennsylvania were on the sea and Kew on the banks of the Thames.

58b

58. James Wyatt (1746-1813)
Shoebury Castle, Essex
Design for a new house
Elevation of south front
Insc. A Plan for Shoebury Castle designed by James Wyatt Esq for
Sir John Smith Burges Bart 1797
Pen and wash (360 x 510)
Lit. & reprd. John Harris, *Georgian Country Houses*, 1968,
pp 52-3
RIBA Drawings Collection

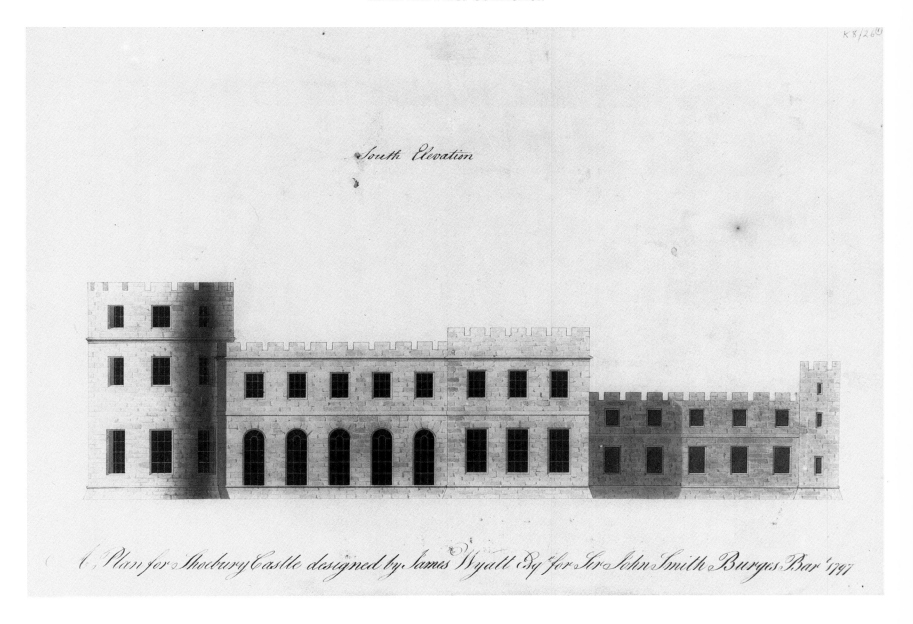

South Elevation

A Plan for Shoebury Castle designed by James Wyatt Esq for Sir John Smith Burges Bart 1797

Beckford began to plan his new 'convent' in June 1796, after his return from Portugal. His first design was less dramatic than the last, and has been called 'Batalha' because it is based upon the reconstruction of the Mausoleum of King John at that Portugese monastery. *59a* is Wyatt's first design for Fonthill. *59b* shows the reconstruction of the Mausoleum of King John I at Batalha, engraved for J.C. Murphy and Luis de Sousa's *Batalha*, 1795.

In fact Wyatt had earlier, in 1782, used the same source for Lee Priory, Kent, obtaining the idea, not from Beckford, but

Beckford took up residence in the southern part of his abbey. Hardly had the whole structure been finished, in February 1819, when the southwestern tower began to crumble and had to be rebuilt. Finally, in 1825 the great tower collapsed, bringing down most of the western hall.

Much has been made of comparing Fonthill with Strawberry Hill, but there is no comparison between these two monuments in the history of the Gothic revival in the matter of volumetric mass and theatrical effect. Beckford's ambition was to build a huge, Mediaeval abbey-church for domestic use, and the more

THE SOUTH ELEVATION of the MAUSOLEUM of KING JOHN I.st at BATALHA.

59b

59a

59c

from his contacts with Colonel Conyngham of Slane Castle, Ireland, who had studied Batalha. Within a year Beckford had moved on to the 'spire' design (*59c*) for in 1797 Joseph Farington reported that 'the Spire of the new Gothic building is to be 300 foot high.' However Beckford and Wyatt had even grander ambitions, for the above perspective (*59*) must represent an enlarged spire design, later rendered into a finished watercolour by Charles Wild (now in the Victoria and Albert Museum, London). The spire was never built and the tower fell down in May 1800. Work began seriously again in 1805 and by 1807

it rivalled Salisbury Cathedral the better. Although Strawberry Hill was a famous house, it was only published in Walpole's rare guide, whereas Fonthill was given mass circulation, by Storer in 1812, and by the two substantial works of Britton and Rutter, both in 1823.

THE PICTURESQUE HOUSE

59. *James Wyatt (1746-1813)*
Fonthill Abbey, Wiltshire
The enlarged spire design
Perspective from the north-west
Pen and wash over pencil (250 x 180)
Lit. & reprd. RIBA Catalogue... The Wyatt Family, ed. Derek Linstrom, 1973; *William Beckford*, catalogue of an exhibition, Bath, 1976, pp 35ff
RIBA DRAWINGS COLLECTION

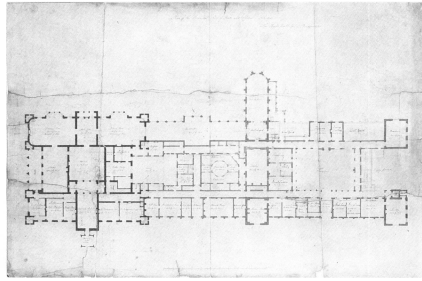

6ob

6oa

Surprisingly, it is Jeffry Wyatt, James's nephew, who first appears at Ashridge, for the 3rd Duke of Bridgewater, but this was to improve the accommodation in a small house in 1803. Then in 1807 James produced the first designs that led eventually to Ashridge as we know it today, and in 1813 Jeffry took over after his uncle's death. With the loss of Fonthill, Ashridge is the only reminder of the huge scale of Beckford's abbey. Unlike Fonthill, Ashridge was perfectly symmetrical as far as the main block was concerned: Wyatt's plan of the ground floor of Ash-ridge (6oa) shows the formal and symmetrical shape of the main body of the house, in darker wash, and the huge extensions, to one side in lighter. Some comparison could be made with Wyatt's Kew Palace of 1801, for George III, a building in the castle style rather than the Mixed Gothic of Ashridge. Although Ashridge was not the father of the typical mixed gothic house of abbatial character, it became an ideal model for the grand house all over Britain, and 6ob shows a watercolour view by J.C. Buckler of the north front.

60. *James Wyatt (1746-1813)*
Ashridge Park, Hertfordshire
Design for the south elevation, with scale
*Insc. Elevation of the South Front of House, Conservatory, and
Chapel/ The Right Honble Earl of Bridgewater*
Pen and wash (410 x 535)
Lit. & reprd. RIBA Catalogue... Wyatt Family, ed. Derek Lind-
strom, 1973, fig. 22
RIBA Drawings Collection

61c

61a

61b

All Lugar's books, especially the *Architectural Sketches for Cottages...*, 1805, make clear his acceptance of the Picturesque theories of Repton and Nash; he even includes examples of Nash's asymmetrical Italianate villa style, with Gold Hill, Kent, 1806. It is not clear how Lugar established a practice in Scotland, but in two pioneering works, both in Dunbartonshire, he introduced the picturesque castle style to a country already enamoured of the symmetrical castle-style buildings of Robert Adam and followers such as John Paterson. Tullichewan Castle, for John Stirling in 1808, and Ballach (now Ardoch) Castle, for John Buchanan in 1809, were each exhibited by Lugar at the Royal Academy in their respective years, as well as in his own books (*61a* is his engraving of the plan of Tullichewan). The house

was demolished in 1954 (*61b & c*).

Lugar's sources are eclectic. Something perhaps of Richard Payne Knight's seminal Downton Castle, Shropshire, of 1772, a little from East Barsham Hall, Norfolk, a celebrated East Anglian Tudor house, something too from James Wyatt's Cassiobury Park, Hertfordshire, of about 1803. And much from a study of John Nash's exhibited drawings at the Royal Academy, especially for Killymoon Castle, in 1803.

61. *Robert Lugar (c. 1773-1855)*
Tullichewan Castle, Dunbartonshire
Perspective design
Pen and watercolour (210 x 350)
Reprd. Robert Lugar, *Plans and Views of Buildings executed in England and Scotland in the Castellated and Other Styles*, 1823, pls 1-6
RIBA DRAWINGS COLLECTION

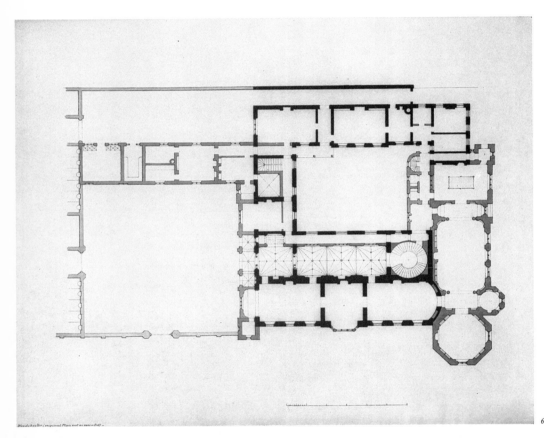

Woodchester (original Plan not as executed)

62a

According to J.N. Brewer's *Delineations of Gloucestershire*, 1825-1827, the old mansion, called Spring Park, seat of Lord Ducie, had 'lately been much improved and enlarged with a new Library, Breakfast Room and Dining-Room, under the direction of J. Adey Repton'. The three rooms are those on the east front as proposed in these two alternative 'flaps'. *62a* shows J.A. Repton's plan for proposed additions in Tudor style at Woodchester, with the existing Georgian house in black wash. A group of three Library rooms are followed by a billiard room. Repton's designs epitomise the Picturesque response to a site, offering the client in this case a choice of styles by means of attached 'before and after' flaps that had been invented by John Adey's father Humphry, the celebrated gardener. Woodchester was demolished in 1846 when William Leigh, the new owner, after consulting A.W.N. Pugin, began a new house in the Viollet-le-Duc style, incomplete in 1858 and remaining as such today on the site of Lord Ducie's house.

62. *John Adey Repton (1775-1860)*
Woodchester Park, Gloucestershire
Designs for re-building part of an older house
Elevation of east front showing a mixed-Gothic castle-style
house, with two attached flaps, one of the old east front (to
the right), the other for an alternative classical design
Pen and watercolour (350 x 510) (flaps 170 x 133)
RIBA DRAWINGS COLLECTION

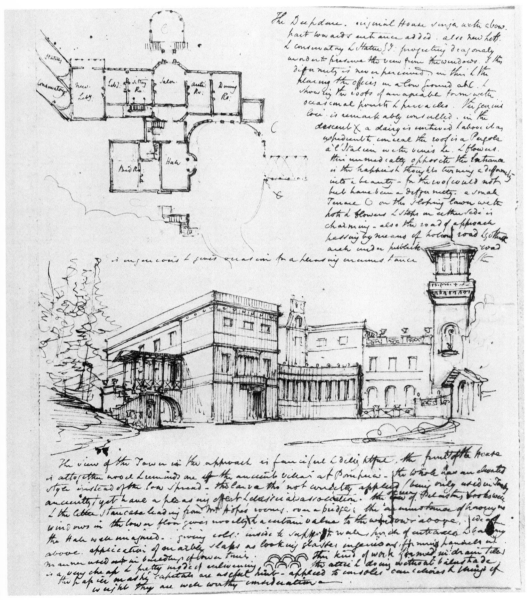

It does not matter that this is the design, made before 1807, for Hope's London Picture Gallery and not one in his country house at The Deepdene, for it perfectly illustrates Hope's Greek idea for interiors. The room was arranged as a temple. The columns supporting the raised skylight were in imitation of those from the Temple of the Winds, the trabeated ceiling came from the Theseum, the four massive Doric columns from the Propylaea, and the façade of the organ from the Erectheion. In his *Household Furniture And Interior Decoration*, 1807, Hope, writing that this room assumed 'the appearance of a sanctuary', described the detailing and iconography of the organ, where the 'car of the god of Music, of Apollo, glides over the center of the pediment. The tripods, sacred to this deity, surmount the angles. Laurel wreaths and other emblems, belonging to the sons of Latona, appear embroidered on the drapery, which, in the form of an ancient *peplum* or veil, descends over the pipes'. In effect the room was a holy of holy's to the Muses.

The drawing is a precious document as to how Hope ordered the execution of his sketched designs, presumably to his architect, who may have been William Atkinson. The reference on the verso to the *rooms where the vases are* is specifically to the 'Room Containing Greek Fictile Vases' (*Household Furniture*, pl. III) where large vases were kept in compartments 'divided by terms, surmounted with heads of the Indian or bearded Bacchus'. One of the most uncompromising attempts to adapt Greek temple forms to an interior, Hope's room must rank as one of the first examples of what would become the approved Greek Revival style for public museums.

C.R. Cockerell visited the Deepdene (*63a*) on 16 August 1823, and wrote in his diary, full of praise, that 'the genius loci is remarkably recalled'. He thought the 'pergola *a italienne* is with vines and flowers... the happiest thought'. 'Novelty has a vast effect in archtr', he further wrote, 'We are sick to see the same thing repeated and over again what has been seen anytime these 100 yrs. The Deepdene attracts in this respect exceeding but if the Pompeian style can be so cultivated as to practice well it may supercede the Templar style in which we have so long worked.'

THE PICTURESQUE HOUSE

63. *Thomas Hope (1769-1831)*
Hope's house in Duchess Street, London
Design for the Picture Gallery
Perspective towards the organ.
Verso: detail of bookcases and of brass railing
Insc. verso, *in the rooms where the vases are,* recto, by Hope, *Large picture gallery* and *The organ white & gold the space between the columns painted as drapery, red — the ornaments gold — The bookcases mahogany & ormolu — see the other side* (of the drawing) *NB The organ & bookcases should be higher in proportion to the room*
Pen (210 x 330)
Lit. David Watkin, *Thomas Hope 1769-1831 and the Neoclassical idea,* 1968
PRIVATE COLLECTION

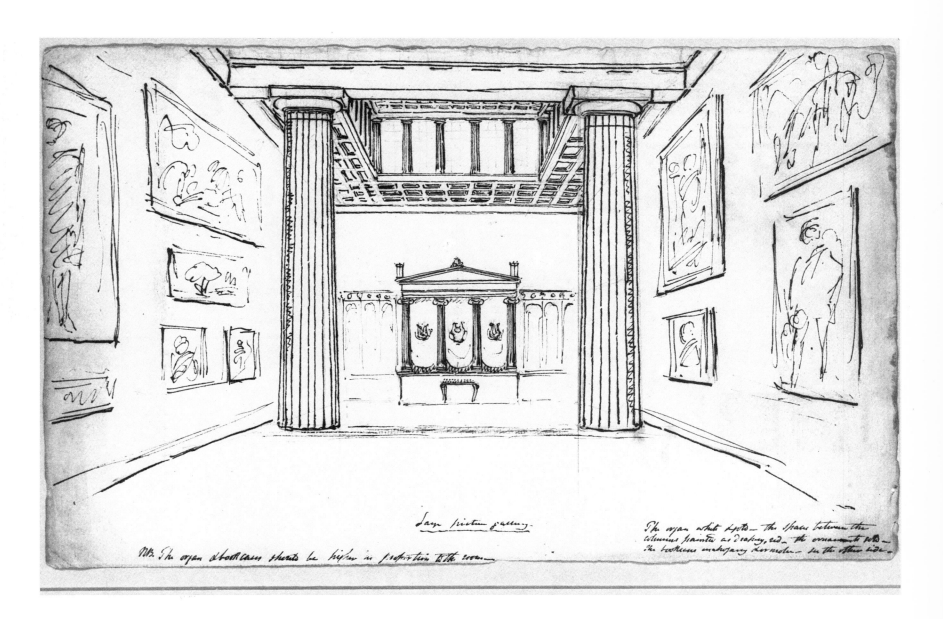

64c

64b

64a

Even before the collapse of Fonthill Abbey, William Beckford had already planned to move to Bath. His choice of architect in 1823 was surprising, for Goodridge was young and untried, except for enlargements to the Argyle Chapel at Bathwick. However, he was quite clearly exceptional, for he is known to have studied in Paris in 1818. For one so young, Lansdown Tower, begun in 1828, was a remarkable accomplishment, for it portrays, in J.M. Crook's words 'that conjunction of Neoclassicism and the Picturesque which was the product of the Romantic age in British architecture'. Not only is it partly neo-Greek, from the Choragic monument of Lysicrates and Tower of the Winds, and Franco-Italian, but there are hints in its detailing of Vanbrugh, who was, as Goodridge recognised, perhaps the first architect to appreciate the Picturesque. The Tower was published by E.F. English and W. Maddox, as *Views of Lansdown Tower, Bath*, 1844, where English coruscated that 'no language can do justice to an object so unique'. It cannot be a coincidence that Thomas Hope's Deepdene, Surrey, the other great monument of asymmetrical Picturesque, was also built for a collector of like taste to Beckford.

Goodridge's linear drawings (*64a* is his elevation of the garden or rear front, showing the bridge for the path that led down the hill to Beckford's house in Royal Crescent, Bath and *64b* the perspective of the Library) cannot be disassociated from Hope's in his *Household Furniture*, 1807, or Percier and Fontaine's *Receuil de décorations intérieurs*, 1801, the latter book purchased by Goodridge in Paris in 1818.

64. Henry Edmund Goodridge (1797-1864)
Lansdown Tower, Bath, Somerset
Design for the entrance front
Pen (465 x 300)
Lit. J. Millington, *Beckford's Tower, Lans-
down*, Bath, 1973; J.M. Crook, *The Greek
Revival*, 1972, pp 102-104; *William Beck-
ford*, catalogue of an exhibition, Bath, 1976,
pp 57-60
RIBA DRAWINGS COLLECTION

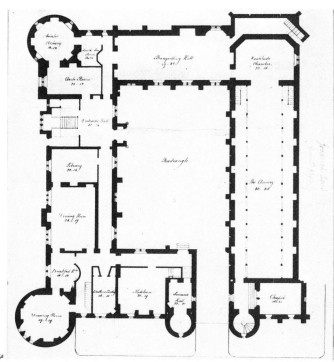

65a

65b

Blore was trained in the antiquarian tradition of topographical draughtsmanship and watercolour painting, hence his great skill in this medium. His friendship with Sir Walter Scott and the ideas he contributed to the building of Abbotsford in Roxburghshire in 1816 probably led to his commissions to build Corehouse in Lanarkshire in 1824 and Freeland House, Perthshire, in 1825. He would soon emerge as a master of a huge range of styles, not unlike his Scottish contemporary William Burn. The commission for Goodrich probably came through the Society of Antiquaries, where Blore had met Dr (later Sir) Samuel Rush Meyrick, who in 1824 had published *A Critical Inquiry into Antient Armour as it existed in Europe*, based upon his own collection, celebrated as the 'most remarkable assemblage of Arms, Armour and Antiquities in the civilized globe'. It was the inadequacy of his house in London that persuaded Meyrick to engage Blore in 1828 to build a modern castle in

proximity to the famous fourteenth-century one that stood nearby. As there is really nothing in Blore's earlier or later career remotely resembling Goodrich, he was clearly the enthusiastic executant of ideas offered by Meyrick, who had travelled through Germany, Austria and Czechoslovakia in 1823 looking at castles. Goodrich was not archaeologically correct in its details; *65a*, the plan of the ground floor of Goodrich in a preliminary design, shows Blore's inability to conceive an authentic Mediaeval arrangement of rooms within a Picturesque exterior, as would have been done by Salvin, for example, and his perspective of the courtyard (*65b*) exudes a collegiate rather than castle air. But the amateur mind that conceived it has given it a senes of realism lacking in earlier revival castles. After Meyrick's death in 1848 it was altered, the collections sold in 1868, and the castle was demolished in 1950.

65. *Edward Blore (1787-1879)*
Goodrich Court, Herefordshire
Perspective
Watercolour (260 x 495)
Lit. Hugh Meller, 'The Architectural History of Goodrich
Court, Herefordshire', *Transactions of the Woolhope Naturalist's
Field Club*, XLII, 1977, pt II
RIBA DRAWINGS COLLECTION

66a

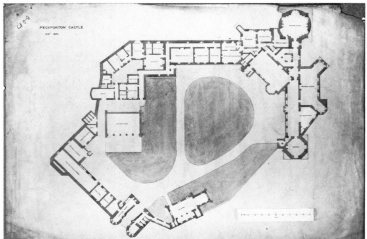

66b

If Goodrich marked the beginning of the making of realistic castles, Peckforton was the beginning of the end, for by the date it was built A.W.N. Pugin had begun to mock such castles, and in 1858 Sir George Gilbert Scott was to attack the 'monstrous practice of castle-building' in his *Remarks on Secular and Domestic Architecture*. Salvin was the best castle builder of his century, 'celebrated', Alfred Waterhouse wrote to Lord Tollemache, in 1878, 'for the way in which he can combine the exterior and plan of an Edwardian castle with nineteenth-century elegance and comfort'. Salvin was able to understand the volumetric mass of castles, and to see in their concentric plan with defensive walls the perfect envelope for his loosely-arranged suites of domestic rooms. His training under John Nash gave him a developed sense of the Picturesque, and this pictorial way of looking cannot be better demonstrated than in his evocative watercolour designs. He was an arch-Victorian architect, yet was adept in combining fine and accurate detail, not too historicist, with fluid, almost free-wheeling plans, that owed more to the relaxed informality of the Regency than to anything by his contemporaries, who were becoming more and more constrained by the formal needs of the Victorian country house.

Peckforton was built from 1844 to 1850, for Lionel (later 1st Lord) Tollemache. *66a* is Salvin's perspective design for the courtyard. A telling comparison may be made between the plan of Goodrich Castle and Peckforton's plan (*66b*, which is dated November 1848).

THE PICTURESQUE HOUSE

66. Anthony Salvin (1799-1881)
Peckforton Castle (Cheshire)
Perspective of outside walls from the south
Watercolour (350 x 550)
Lit. & reprd. Mark Girouard, *The Victorian Country House*, 1971,
pp 73-7; pls 113-4
RIBA DRAWINGS COLLECTION

THE PICTURESQUE HOUSE

When in 1837 Edward Hussey decided to build a new house, he stabilised the old moated castle in the valley by converting it into a picturesque ruin in the park, and then built the Tudor-style house on top of the hill (67a). He could not have chosen a better architect than Salvin, who was the last great master of the Picturesque tradition. There is no doubt that Salvin regarded Scotney as a great achievement, and it is surely significant that this Royal Academy exhibit of 1838 was prepared by two professional artists; James Deason for the architecture, and George Arthur Fripp for the landscape and figures. 67b is Salvin's own plan of the ground floor of Scotney, showing the new house sited on formal terraces overlooking the romantic park.

67a

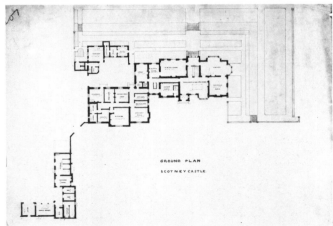

GROUND PLAN
SCOTNEY CASTLE

67b

THE PICTURESQUE HOUSE

67. *Anthony Salvin*
Scotney Castle, Kent
View towards the entrance front
Perspective
Watercolour (555 x 775)
Lit. & reprd. Gavin Stamp, *The Great Perspectivists*, 1982, 46,
fig. 36; Jill Lever & Margaret Richardson, *The Art of the Archi-
tect*, 1984, 93, pl. 74
RIBA DRAWINGS COLLECTION

68. *Samuel Beazley (1786-1851)*
Bretby Park, Derbyshire
Design for the Countess of Chesterfield's Boudoir
Interior perspective, presented in a simulated frame
Pen and watercolour (410 x 355)
RIBA DRAWINGS COLLECTION

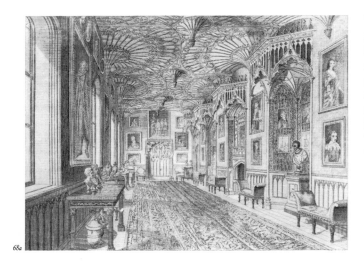

68a

The 5th Earl of Chesterfield began to build a new mansion at Bretby by 1813, in the process demolishing one of the grandest houses of the seventeenth century. Sir Jeffry Wyattville and others were involved. In 1838 Samuel Beazley exhibited this design for the Countess's Boudoir, but it is unclear if it was ever executed. With its fan-vaulting, its all-over cosmetic of cusped panelling, this design can be regarded as an end of the line product of Gothic interiors, that began with Horace Walpole's at Strawberry Hill, Middlesex (*68a*), progressing via William Porden's at Eaton Hall, Cheshire in 1804.

THE PICTURESQUE HOUSE

6*9a*   6*9b*

Harlaxton is one of the most spectacular houses in England, the creation of Gregory Gregory, a bachelor who devoted all his fortune and energies to its building. The invention is almost certainly Gregory's, the assemblage Salvin's, at least until Salvin was dismissed in 1837, when William Burn took over. J.C. Loudon came to Harlaxton in May 1840, and claims of Gregory that 'from entering so completely into both the design and the practical details of execution he may be said to have embodied himself in the edifice, and to live in every feature of it'. To accomplish this Gregory travelled to all the celebrated Elizabethan or Jacobean houses in England, and in 1831 summoned Salvin to 'embody' his ideas in such detail as to fit them for the practical builder'. The visual power and strength of Harlaxton is in the synthesis. Just as many of the latter additions to Harlaxton under Burn (or his assistant David Bryce) were of a decided South German Baroque character, so does Harlaxton strike one as Baroque by virtue of its modelling. In planning it is still astonishingly free, and Picturesque qualities are apparent in the drawings—6*9a* is his design for the east or side front, dated 1831, and 6*9b*, a view of the entrance front of Harlaxton seen from the upper terrace—among all Salvin's surviving designs, the best ones, most carefully shadowed and modulated. Just how important this job was to Salvin is shown by *tour de forces* in the shape of four surviving perspectives in a private collection, themselves masterpieces of the perspectivist's art.

69. *Anthony Salvin (1799-1881)*
Harlaxton Hall, Lincolnshire
Design for the northern entrance front, with scale
Insc. The North elevation of Harlaxton Manor S. A. Salvin archt
som. st
Pen and watercolour (515 x 750)
Lit & reprd. Mark Girouard, *The Victorian Country House*, 1979,
pp 90-102, pl. 61
RIBA Drawings Collection

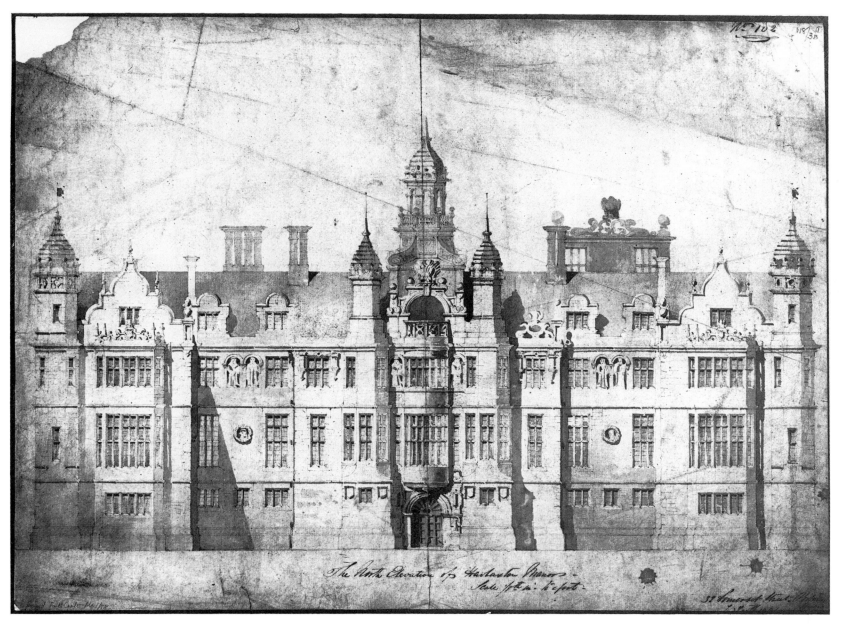

Pugin's patron at Scarisbrick was Charles Scarisbrick, who summoned him to rebuild and enlarge the existing house in 1836. Pugin was to be assiduously drawing until 1845. His great achievement was the creation of the Mediaeval hall, conceived in 1836 but not completed until 1842. Pugin's design for the Great Hall at Scarisbrick (70a), his *beau-ideal* translated with immediacy into a convincing perspective, shows how he did not work with preliminary sketches, but, like Lutyens, later spelt out the final product in one creative process. His first design for Scarisbrick, (70b), included a clock tower with chapel, which would only be built later, by E.W. Pugin, in a more muscular style.

His design must be considered as a lode-star in the revival of the Elizabethan Great Hall. As for precedent, Salvin was restoring the Mediaeval hall at Brancepath Castle, Durham, in 1829, and his huge Jacobean hall at Harlaxton is dated 1833. In 1836 Pugin also conceived his hall at Alton Towers, Staffordshire, about which he wrote to his patron that he must have 'a bay window, high open roof, two good fireplaces, a great sideboard, screen, minstrel gallery—all or none'. There was also

70b

70a

70c

the splendid baronial hall at Bayons Manor, Lincolnshire, and this, as at Scarisbrick (70c shows the house in 1963) and at Alton Towers, is essentially identified in the general composition of the house by the prominent roof.

THE PICTURESQUE HOUSE

70. *Augustus Welby Northmore Pugin (1812–1852)*
Scarisbrick Hall, Lancashire
Design for the chimney-piece in the Great Hall
Elevation, seen in perspective
Signed & dated. AW Pugin 1836
Watercolour (320 x 225)
Lit. Mark Girouard, The Victorian Country House, 1979, 43-4; 110-19: and for the complicated history of the Hall see *RIBA Catalogue... Pugin*, ed. A. Wedgwood, 1977, 75
RIBA DRAWINGS COLLECTION

71a

71b

Barry's patron was the 3rd Earl of Carnarvon and, as he was a younger branch of the Herberts of Wilton, it was appropriate that in May 1838 Barry first offered a design in a Palladian style, a twinning of Jonesian elements to Palladio's Palazzo Porto. Two years later Barry produced a second design, richer and decidedly Italianate, in the English Elizabethan tradition of Wollaton, called by Early Victorians 'Anglo-Italianate'. The elevations are based on a grid system, and it is no coincidence that at exactly this time Barry was working out the same grid system, but in Gothic, for the Houses of Parliament. The intri-cacy and lace-like quality of much surface ornament, and in particular the terminations above the roof-line and the central tower, mirror the fondness of patrons and architects alike for elaborate Late Gothic, and, on Lord Carnarvon's own part, for the Alhambra. The private chapel in the style of Wren or Gibbs was never built and stylistically is a surprising adjunct: 71b shows the house now. This magnificent perspective was rendered by Thomas Allom and exhibited at the Royal Academy. Barry's neo-Palladian design, (71a) was also a watercolour by Thomas Allorn, dated May 1838.

71. *Sir Charles Barry (1795-1860)*
Highclere Castle, Hampshire
Design for remodelling the old house
Perspective from the north east
Watercolour (495 x 940)
Lit. & reprd. Mark Girouard, *The Victorian Country House*, 1979,
pp 130-37 & pl. XI; Gavin Stamp, *The Great Perspectivists*,
1982, fig. 37
RIBA DRAWINGS COLLECTION

72a

The interior of Barry's great house, begun in 1840, was unfinished when the 3rd Earl of Carnarvon died in 1849. In fact, it was not until the 4th Earl married in 1861 that work was begun again. In 1862 Allom exhibited at the Royal Academy an 'Interior of the Hall at Highclere Castle', which can be identified with this design (72), a highly artistic and swish watercolour by one of the wizard perspectivists of the Victorian age. A writer in the *Civil Engineer and Architect's Journal* for 1862 commented upon 'an artistic composition, if we regard only the general effect', but in a critical tone also observed 'a close scrutiny betrays questionable details'. In fact, he was affronted by the old-fashioned Early Victorian style and the sort of hall that Pugin had done better at Scarisbrick in 1836.

72a is Charles Barry Jnr.'s perspective of the proposed hall at Clumber Park, Nottinghamshire, made after the fire of 1879 and possibly exhibited by Barry (1823-1900) at the Royal Academy in 1880. It is a Classical, Roman response to Allom's Gothic hall—more a public interior than a domestic one, befitting a Duke of monstrous wealth.

72. *Thomas Allom (1804-1872)*
Highclere Castle, Hampshire
Design for the completion of the entrance hall
Perspective
Pencil and watercolour (980 x 650)
RIBA DRAWINGS COLLECTION

73a

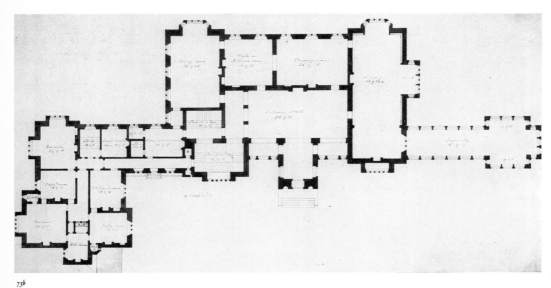

73b

Burn commanded a huge practice; indeed so huge that he can sometimes be accused of aspiring to no more than facile competence. By 1840 he had built more than 90 country houses, 30 churches and 25 public buildings, and he was only 51 years of age! Nevertheless he was wondrously versatile, able to do almost any style asked, and he it was who established in Scotland the fully developed Scottish Baronial style, although the real master of this would be his pupil David Bryce. Stoke Rochford Hall was built for Christopher Turnor from 1839 to 1841, and here Burn provided what he was best at; something efficiently planned and agreeable, without being showy or ostentatious. Burn trained first under Sir Robert Smirk, and then from 1811 in Edinburgh, which marked him out as a follower of the eclectic Picturesque tradition. All Burn's houses took advantage of current progress in drainage or domestic requirements, so that Stoke Rochford was exceptional at that time in having 15 water-closets. Stoke Rochford sits upon a ridge, its main body symmetrical and balanced by a family wing to one side, linked to lower, dependent stables. 73a is Burn's perspective design for the entrance front of Stoke Rochford. The standard conservatory extends from the other side of the house and, as can be seen from 73b, the plan of Stoke Rochford, dated 9 December 1839, the Library opens off the conservatory. The drawing room and billiard room face on to the garden, with the dining-room at the far end, placed conveniently next to the dining service room with easy access to the servants' stairs and kitchen below. All the guest bedrooms were placed upstairs, quite separate from the Turnor's bedroom apartments in the private wing. The style is 'Jacobethan', in the approved Manorial manner, and inside Burn provided much carved woodwork and plasterwork in strapwork style. However, Stoke is a tame house, compared to Harlaxton nearby (69), where Burn had replaced Salvin as architect from 1839.

73. *William Burn (1789-1870)*
Stoke Rochford, Lincolnshire
Design for new house
Perspective of the front from the garden
Watercolour (160 x 484)
RIBA DRAWINGS COLLECTION

74b

74a

In that Hardwick represents the average in Victorian country house architecture, his country houses are likewise average and unspectacular. This Addington design (74), made in about 1856 for Lord Addington in 1887 has the virtue of possessing what one expects of a Victorian house: asymmetry, spiky Gothic detail, and a picturesque grouping of the lower offices, with dairy and kitchen set around a courtyard. There is already a perceptible movement away from the pretty, effeminate look of much Early Victorian Gothic towards the more vigorous, brutalist High Victorian.

Hardwick's perspectives are always highly finished and aesthetically richly presented, in this case for exhibition at the Royal Academy in 1856. An old photograph of the garden front (74a) shows the house as built, to designs modified and altered from the exhibited perspective. 74b shows the staircase and staircase hall. Addington was demolished in about 1928 and a new house built to designs by Michael Waterhouse.

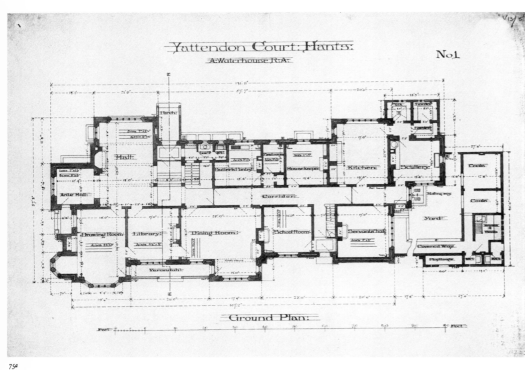

Yattendon Court: Hants:

A: Waterhouse R: A:

No 1

Ground Plan:

75ª

Waterhouse's enormous practice enabled him to buy the Yattendon Estate and build his own house as Lord of the Manor. The design (75) is an example of the type of Victorian house that has so often been censured. The use of a hard, red brick, hard-edged stone dressings and terracotta decorations, materials favoured by Waterhouse for his public buildings, has never been received sympathetically. The ground-floor plan of Yattendon (75a, no. 1 of a set of working drawings) shows how Waterhouse, although a wealthly architect, was only a squire and has given himself a house suited for limited entertaining. Beyond the 'green baize door', across the passage between the butler's pantry and dining-room, occupies nearly two-thirds of the plan. The style is predominantly Tudor Gothic, but with hints of Old English and even early Mediaeval in the tower. Devey would have treated such a tower quite differently (80). Yattendon was replaced by a new house in 1926.

75. *Alfred Waterhouse (1830-1908)*
Yattendon Court, Berkshire
Design for the architect's own house
Perspective
Signed. & dated. A Waterhouse 1878
Watercolour (440 x 550)
RIBA Drawings Collection

Elvetham is an extreme example, and perhaps the best one, of a country house built in the 'streaky bacon style'. It stands as a protest against the conventional smoothness of what was regarded as the jaded classical style, and is the architectural equivalent of muscular Christianity. Teulon was one of the best exponents of this structural polychromy, and built Elvetham, in a hard, red brick patterned with black, between 1859 and 1862 for Lord Calthorpe, who had made a considerable fortune from owning Edgbaston, a prosperous suburb of Birmingham. Teulon's connection with Calthorpe was one of long standing.

He had built the schools at Elvetham, exhibiting his design at the Royal Academy in 1849, and in 1853 exhibited his designs for St James's, Edgbaston, a church in Lord Calthorpe's patronage. The design for the entrance front at Elvetham (76b) was exhibited in 1860.

This sort of style contributed to the later image of the 'unlovely' Victorian house, and it can be said of Elvetham, seen from the entrance approach (76a), that beyond the disintegration of the composition, nothing could be more belligerent and wayward.

76. Samuel Sanders Teulon (1812-1873)
Elvetham Hall (Hampton)
Design for new house
Perspective of the garden side
Watercolour
Lit. Mark Girouard, *The Victorian Country House*, 1979, pp 57-
58, pl. 29 (illustrating two contract drawings) & colour pl. III
(the entrance front, companion to above)
ELVETHAM HALL LIMITED

Knightshayes was built for Sir John Heathcote-Amory Bt, a lace-making magnate. Unusually, he built it as a completely new house on a newly-acquired estate, but by the time the foundations were laid in 1869 it was already apparent that Heathcote-Amory would not be able to afford Burges's expensive and highly technicolour decoration, although some were actually begun and then discontinued. In the Drawing Room, as here (77) in the design for the Library, Burges created his own fantastic world, a dream of revived Mediaevalism. Alas, as Dr Mordaunt Crook remarks, these 'magical interiors remained a half-formed dream' only to re-appear in different, although equally fantastic, form at Cardiff Castle (c. 1871) and Castell Coch (1875). 77a shows the garden front of Knightshayes.

77. *William Burges (1827-1881)*
Knightshayes, Devon
Design for the library
Elevation of chimney wall with half plans of chimney jambs
Insc. Knightshayes No 18 Library Half Inch Scale
Pen and wash (445 x 640)
Lit. J. Mordaunt Crook, *William Burges and the High Victorian Dream*, 1981, pp 302-05
RIBA Drawings Collection

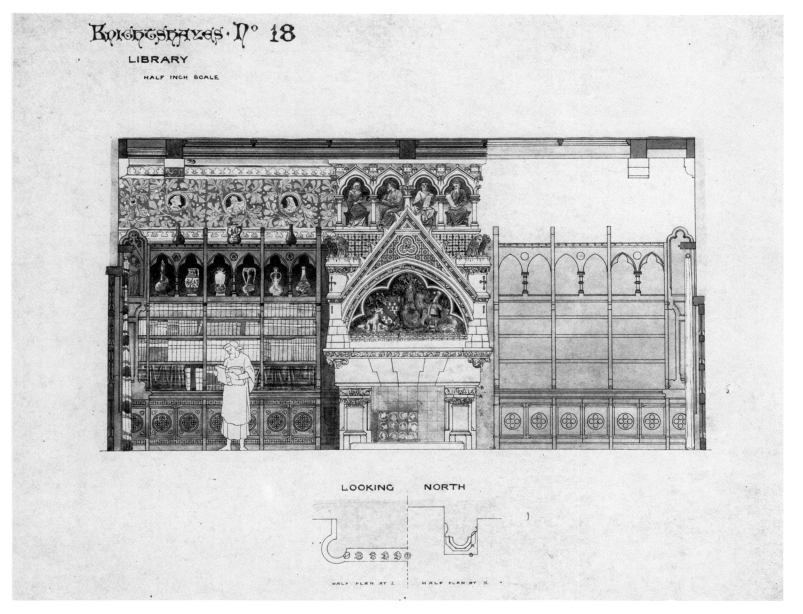

78. John Hungerford Pollen (1820-1902)
Blickling Hall, Norfolk
Design for the Library chimney-piece
Perspective elevation
Signed JHP
Watercolour over pencil and pen (395 x 332)
Lit. & reprd.. Geoffrey Fisher & Helen Smith, 'John Hunger-ford Pollen and his Decorative Work at Blickling Hall', *The National Trust Yearbook 1975-76*, fig. 4
RIBA DRAWINGS COLLECTION

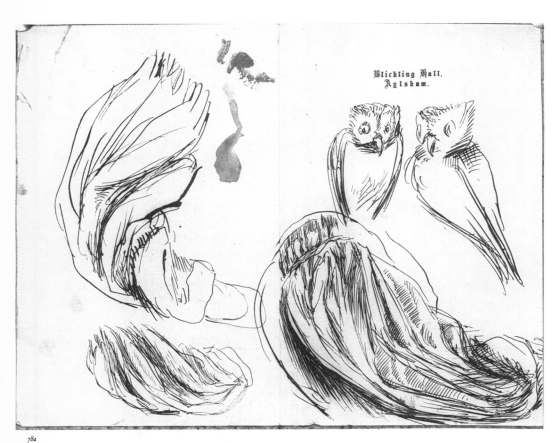

Blickling Hall.
Aglsham.

78a

Pollen has been an undervalued figure in the history of nineteenth-century mural painting and the decorative arts of the interior. As a major contributor to the formation of the Arts and Crafts Exhibition Society in 1887, and as a friend of the Pre-Raphaelites, Pollen can be regarded as a parallel force to that of William Morris.

Lord Lothian inherited Blickling in 1850, and at first employed R.S. Stanhope for the decorations, all of which have disappeared. Pollen was then employed from 1859 to 1861. In his first works of 1859 there is a definite allusion to Celtic sources, absorbed during Pollen's Professorship of Fine Arts at the Catholic University in Dublin between 1854 and 1857. The drawings for the Library at Blickling (*78*) are dated 1859 and 1860, and here Pollen was enriching an early seventeenth- and eighteenth-century room with a frieze that hints of illuminated manuscript decoration. In 1861 he provided the most extraordi-nary chimney-piece, one that would not have looked out of place in Finland in the later nineteenth century. *78a* is a sheet of vigorous sketches by Pollen for decorating, with owls, the gallery frieze, drawn on Blickling Hall notepaper.

79a

79. John Diblee Crace (1838-1919)
Longleat House, Wiltshire
Design for the ceiling of the State Dining-Room
Insc. on verso of mount, see below
Watercolour (495 x 530)
RIBA DRAWINGS COLLECTION

The firm of Fredrick Crace & Son, founded by Frederick Crace, the brilliant decorator of the Brighton Pavilion, was continued through the nineteenth century by his son John Gregory (1809-1889) and then by John Gregory's son John Diblee. Both son and grandson could turn out almost any style requested, although they preferred the Renaissance or Antique Roman style. Hundreds of houses, clubs and public buildings were decorated by the firm, always competently although sometimes with boring precision. There were special exceptions, for special clients, notably the rich sequence of apartments at Longleat, decorated from 1873 to 1880 for the 4th Marquess of Bath. These comprised the Ante-Library, Green Library, Red Library, little Dining-Room, Lower Dining-Room, Saloon, Drawing Room and State Dining-Room. Lord Bath had travelled to Venice in 1875 where he admired the rich decorations of the Doge's Palace and acquired some original ceiling paintings, as well as commissioning Domenico Caldara to make copies of more Venetian Renaissance painting of the Veronese sort. Crace skillfully assembled these into his Venetian-styled interiors (79a), including doors and chimney-pieces copied from originals in the Doge's Palace. A note, copied from an original, on the mount of this drawing (79) describes its origin in detail: *about 1875 the Marquis of Bath purchased in Venice 9 paintings of the sixteenth century, taken from the ceiling panels of some private palace—these were a long octagon as centre & four square panels, all in colour, and four L shaped panels in monochrome. These he requested me to continue in a design for a ceiling of Venetian Character, with such additions as I found necessary. The ceiling so designed was duly carried out in the State Dining Room at Longleat. The Drawing represents rather more than half that ceiling & was made after its completion (s.) J.D. Crace.*

Although by no means a rule, the Craces recognized that Dukes and Marquesseses demanded a regal Renaissance style. Unless a patron was particularly discerning and demanding, the gentry or minor nobility received the standard Crace treatment, mass-produced, like wallpaper.

An understanding of the basis of Devey's style can be gained from the village of Penshurst in Kent. Accompanying a group of fifteenth-century, half-timbered houses with tile-hanging and plaster infill are others in the same style, using the same techniques. But the latter were built by Devey from 1850, and are what we would describe as in the local vernacular, an attempt to reproduce what early builders might have assembled in an apparently accidental way. Macharioch, begun but never completed for the Marquis of Lorne from 1873 and now demolished, was intended to reproduced subtly the artless accretion of centuries, as if the house had grown since the sixteenth century. Nevertheless, Devey's designs (*8o*), like Blore's appealing perspectives, were always better on paper than in the reality (*8oa*). His sensitive watercolour, with its transparent delicacy, is a mark of Devey's artistic training under J.D. Harding and John Cotman, both watercolourists who depicted ancient buildings.

80. *George Devey (1820-1886)*
Macharioch House, Kintyre
Design for a new house
Sketch elevation
Pencil and watercolour (230 x 510)
RIBA Drawings Collection

Sketch Elevation

81a

Nesfield's background was William Burn's office from 1851 to 1853, and his uncle Salvin's from 1853 to 1856. He set up in practice on his own in 1860, beginning his celebrated partnership with Richard Norman Shaw in 1862, which was dissolved in 1868. Between them they effected a revolution in English domestic architecture by reviving the Tudor, Gothic and Elizabethan models with what became known as the Old English Style. Devey had already been doing this for ten years, but he was a shy man and no self-publicist, so that it was left to Nesfield and Shaw to make real capital (in both senses of the word) out of an architecture that was regarded as essentially English: tile-hanging, carved timberwork, leaded lights, moulded seventeenth-century chimney stacks and so forth. It was artistic, and artistry was applied to the decoration of the interiors. In fact, it is as much Arts and Crafts as anything more properly associated with that Movement. Old English and Arts and Crafts are a continuum. Babbacombe, now the Cliff Hotel, was an early nineteenth-century house altered in the 1890s. Nesfield's conversion was of an existing wing (81), possibly old stables, and the new porch. It is dated 1878. 81a, another of the contract drawings, deals with the gable over the archway or 'Approach' and provides in its upper sections samples of material stuffs for wall coverings. The drawing is signed by George Whiffen and Sons, the builders. Note the chimneypiece, inscribed 'East and West Home's Best'.

81. William Eden Nesfield (1835-1888)
Babbacombe Cliff, Devon
Contract design for the addition of new wing
Sheet with four elevations and section, with scale
*Signed & dated. W. Eden Nesfield, 19 Margaret Street, Cavendish
Square, London W. 1877*
Lit. RIBA Catalogue... L-W, 1973, ed. Jill Lever, p. 113
RIBA DRAWINGS COLLECTION

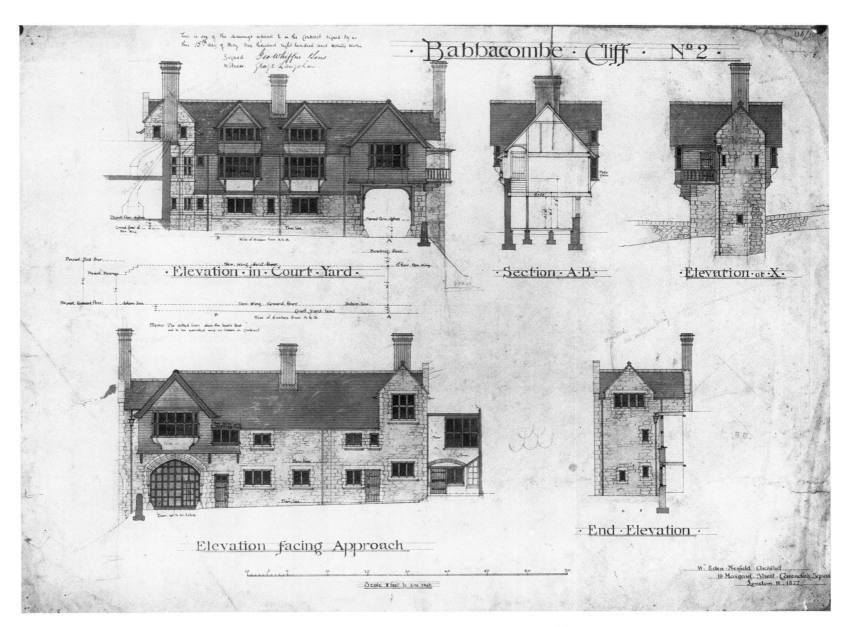

82a

Grim's Dyke, named because the old prehistoric way crossed the site, was built 1870-1872 for the Academician painter Frederick Goodhall. When exhibited at the Royal Academy in 1872, this drawing (*82*) was described in *Building News* as 'an artistic house by an artist for an artist'. The conception of an 'artistic' house demanded attention to the minutest detail, hence Shaw's artfully picturesque Old English style with its tile-hung gables, elaborate carved and incised woodwork, and glass set in leaded lights, an exposition of the arts of the crafts-man. Out of all this emerged the Arts and Crafts Movement. The curious juxtaposition of axes, seen dramatically in this perspective was due to Goodhall's requirement that he have a studio with a north light, whereas he wanted the main body of the house (seen to the left of the view) to sit along the Grim's Dyke itself. This is one of Shaw's finest drawings. In contrast to contemporary pictorial practice, it is minimal and economic of line, for Shaw deplored highly coloured presentations with figures of 'well-dressed ladies and gentlemen', and was never persuaded to include such alluring incidentals in his drawings. H.S. Goodhart-Rendel thought there was little in Shaw's draw-ings to 'captivate but a very thorough attempt to explain'. This drawing is not unlike Shaw's Royal Academy presentation piece, a drawing of his more famous Leyswood in Sussex, (*82a*), inscribed *R. Norman Shaw delt 1868*. Leyswood, near Groom-bridge, Sussex, was made for James William Temple. With this drawing and a companion one Shaw made his debut at the Royal Academy in 1870. Demolished in 1950, Leyswood was one of the most serious post-war country house losses.

82. Richard Norman Shaw (1831-1912)
Grim's Dyke, Middlesex
Design for a new house
Perspective of back of house from south-east
Pen (495 x 670)
Lit. & reprd. Gavin Stamp, *The Great Perspectivists*, 1982, fig.
78; Jill Lever & Margaret Richardson, *The Art of the Architect*,
1984, p. 13, pl. 99
RIBA Drawings Collection

THE VICTORIAN & EDWARDIAN HOUSE

Beauvale was not the seat of a family in the sense of an ancestral home, but was built because the 7th Earl Cowper owned vast coal fields and acreages in Nottinghamshire, inherited without a house. Mark Girouard aptly describes Godwin and William Burges as the Castor and Pollux of Victorian architecture, both building 'romantic, richly wrought and highly impracticable Gothic buildings'. By the time Godwin obtained the Beauvale commission in 1871 he had designed, in 1866, an impractical and vast fortified castle at Dromore in Ireland. By 1871 he was becoming acutely aware of the growing strength of Devey and Shaw and the Old English style. Beauvale encapsulates both this and Godwin's romantic 'Dromoric' yearnings. The site was in the middle of a forest, and this inspired the tall tower from which one could look out across the tree-tops. Unlike Devey whose houses tend to sit firmly and comfortably, as if sprawling on the ground, Godwin has built his lively composition up into a pyramid, the steep French-like roofs giving it a Gothic effect, seen in *83a*, a photolithograph from the *Building News*, July 3, 1874, of Beavale as completed.

83. Edward William Godwin (1833-1886)
Beauvale Lodge, Nottinghamshire
Design for new house
Perspective from the west
Watercolour (425 x 510)
Lit. & reprd. Mark Girouard, *The Victorian Country House*, 1976,
pp 329-335, pl. 316
RIBA DRAWINGS COLLECTION

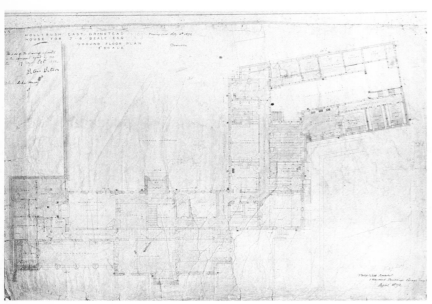

84a

84b

The inscription on *84* refers to the Hollybush Estate that J.S. Beale, a successful London solicitor, had bought in Sussex. Webb was approached for designs, and after many revisions, the contract drawings were finally signed in October 1892 (the contract drawing plan of the ground floor (*84a*) dated April 1892). His new house was in effect an addition, although a large one, to the existing sixteenth-century tile-hung farmhouse, and it was this local Sussex Wealden building tradition that inspired Webb to combine into one whole a variety of parts and textures of material that had taken his eye elsewhere. Thus there are shallow segment-headed windows set in brick walls of late seventeenth-century type, both weather-boarded and tile-hung gables, exterior plasterwork, rough-casting, and brick and stone patterned infills. The end-product, seen in *84b* in an old photograph, is like a farm house that has grown just a little too self-consciously. Devey, for example, would have produced a more artless effect in drawing, but less artistic in the finishing.

84. *Philip Webb (1831-1915)*
Standen, Sussex
Contract design
Elevations of south front and elevation of north front with section
through west wing
Insc. Hollybush East Grinstead House for J. B. Beale Esq
Signed & dated. Philip Webb architect and contractually, 17 October 1892
Pen and coloured wash (505 x 745)
Lit. Mark Girouard, The Victorian Country House
RIBA DRAWINGS COLLECTION

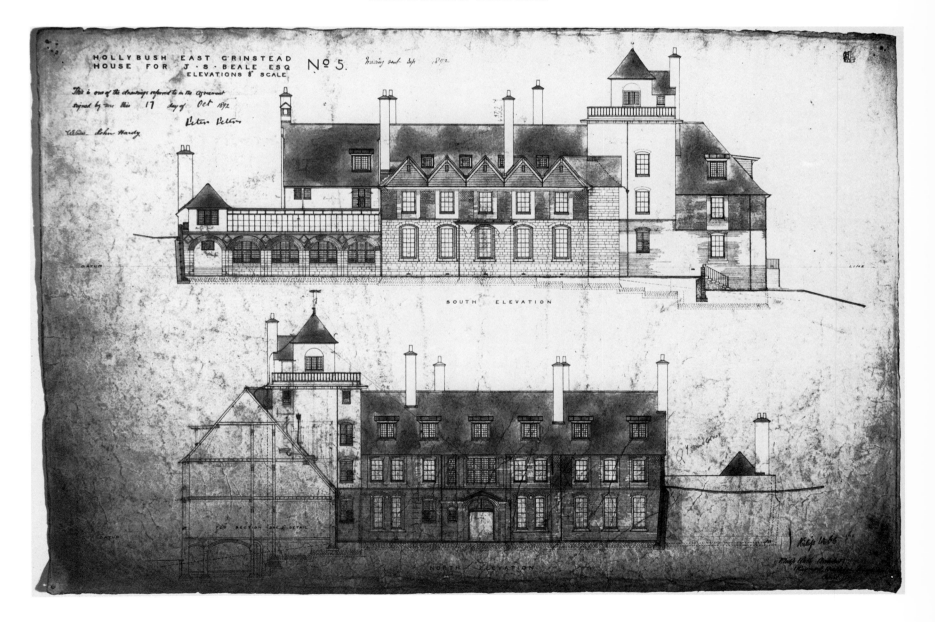

Axel Haig came to Scotland from Sweden in 1856 as a ship-builder. Ten years later he had become a fully-fledged architect, but he was first and foremost a draughtsman, and a wizard one at that. From 1867 he was regularly producing work for *The Building News*. In a way he became to William Burges what J.M. Gandy had been to Sir John Soane, the amanuensis of his dreams. Many other architects were indebted to him, including the unknown architect of this pair of perspectives of a design for a country house in the Old English style (*85 & 85a*, the latter being of the entrance front). Indeed, in 1868 Haig had published in *The Building News* a view of Sir George Lea's half-timbered house at Bagshot in Surrey, already demonstrating the growing interest in a style that would reach creative heights in the work of Devey, Shaw and Webb. This unidentified house is an astonishing evocation of the black and white half-timbered style prevalent in Shropshire and Lancashire: such a house might have featured in the painted imaginary compositions of Atkinson Grimshaw.

85. *Axel Herman Haig (1835-1912)*
Design for a half-timbered house in the Old English style
Perspective from the garden
Signed & dated. A.H.H. 1873
Watercolour (420 x 540)
RIBA DRAWINGS COLLECTION

THE VICTORIAN & EDWARDIAN HOUSE

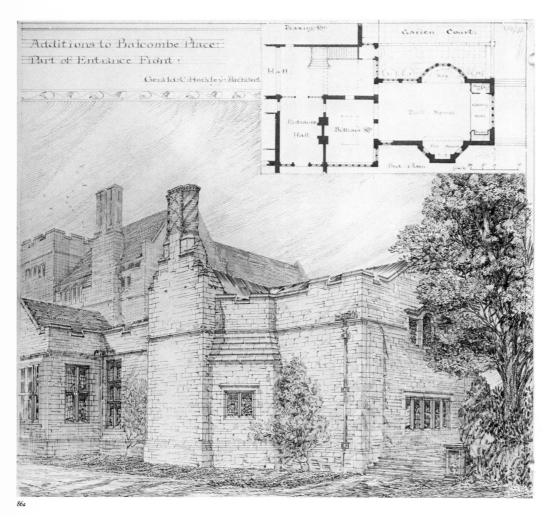

Additions to Balcombe Place:
Part of Entrance Front:

Gerald C Horsley Architect

86a

Balcombe Place had been designed in the Tudor Style by Henry Clutton in the 1850s. Horsley followed this style for the music room built onto the house in 1899, but inside created one of the most perfect ensembles of the Arts and Crafts Movement (86). The design for the Ball Room (86a) shows the exterior with the Clutton house rising behind and a plan of the addition that included an entrance hall and billiard room.

Horsley was one of the founders of the Art Workers' Guild, and his essay on 'The Union of Art' in *Architecture, a Profession or an Art* in 1892 advocated the merging of the arts of painting, decoration and carving with architecture. He had been articled to Richard Norman Shaw in 1879 and was the son of J.C. Horsley, a painter. As Arthur Keen recollected, 'he could draw intricate vaulting or tracery with the utmost precision and firmness, or could make beautiful studies of sculptured detail in which the most sensitive accuracy was combined with soft, refined texture'.

86. *Gerald Callcott Horsley (1862-1917)*
Balcombe Place (Sussex)
Design for the Music Room
Perspective of interior
Insc. The Music Gallery : Balcombe Place
Signed. Gerald C. Horsley Architect
Sepia pen (420 x 550)
Lit. & reprd. Margaret Richardson, *Architects of the Arts and Crafts Movement*, 1981, pp 30-31, pl. 26
RIBA Drawings Collection

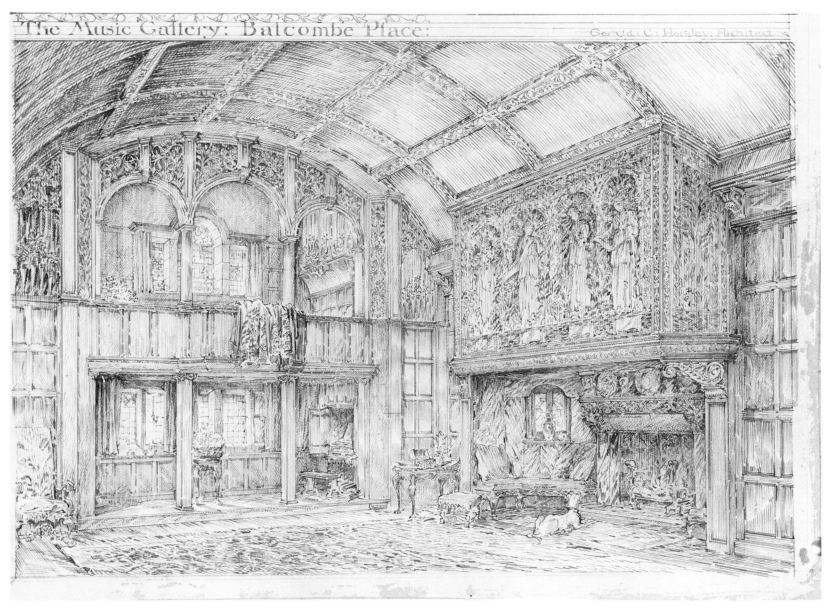

The Music Gallery: Balcombe Place: Gerald C. Horsley Architect

87a

In a way Buchan Hill (87) is the epitome of what a *nouveau-riche* Victorian house ought to be. It is flamboyant, rich, externally prepossessing, somehow bespeaking wealth through trade. Its owner, P. Saillard, was an ostrich feather manufacturer, and for him in 1882-83 George and Peto provided the best example of what can be described as their Harrington Gardens style, for this hot, red brick, yellow stone, terracotta details, executed in a Flemish Renaissance style, can be found along Harrington Gardens in London where they built a number of grand town houses. In his obituary appreciation of George in *The Builder* in 1922, E. Guy Dawber wrote that he was 'an able and brilliant planner, and the ease with which his buildings grouped together in the particularly picturesque manner he made his own never ceased to excite our keen appreciation'. George's genius was to be able to think volumetrically right from the first, constructing a finished perspective not as the end product of a period of creation, but at the beginning. Later, this 'worm's eye view' as Sir Edwin Lutyens called it when he was in George's office, would be transferred to plan, elevation and section for the preparation of contract drawings for the builder. Another characteristic job is here shown (87a) in Sir Ernest George's and Alfred B. Yeates's design for the addition of a new wing to North Mymms House, Herefordshire, in 1894 for Walter H. Burns, which is a most sympathetic extension in an Elizabethan manorial style that nearly doubled the size of the house, as the block plan shows.

87. *Sir Ernest George (1839-1922) & Harold Peto (1884-1933)*
Buchan Hill, Sussex
Design for a new house
Perspective of the entrance front with ground plan
Insc. Buchan Hill Sussex| for P. Saillard Esqr|Ernest George &
Peto Archts
Sepia pen, wash and watercolour (425 x 830)
Lit. Mark Girouard, *The Victorian Country House*
RIBA Drawings Collection

George and Peto exhibited drawings for Poles at the Royal Academy in 1890 and 1891: the plasterwork over the chimney-piece is dated the latter year. The Poles design (88) is a very successful evocation of a Jacobean room and this type of natural-istic, or super-real, interior is typical of George who was cleverly adept at arranging furniture and objects 'to add warm and lovely colour to the beauty of the surroundings' (Darcy Braddell in *The Builder*, CLXVIII, 1945, p.6). Not surprisingly this was the period that saw the rise of the professional antique dealer and the establishment of antique shops. Pieces of furniture were

88a

88b

sought that seemed fitting for an ensemble. Nothing in this room needed to have come down to the owner through family inheritance. The same approach can be seen at Edgeworth Manor Gloucestershire (88b), rebuilt by George for Arthur J. James in 1899 in a mixture of Tudor and Renaissance. Inside he created his idea of a Mediaeval Great Hall. Like Poles, this room would probably have been furnished from antique shops, and the chimney-piece might well have been an original one imported from France.

88a shows Poles, in a photograph from the lawn taken in about 1920. *The Building News* reported in May 1890 that 'Messrs

Ernest George and Peto's chief work shown this year is a country house called Poles, Hertfordshire, for Mr E.S. Hanbury'. Edmund Smith Hanbury (1850-1913) had succeeded to the estate in 1884. For him and his wife, George built a comfortable house in the English Jacobean gabled style, owing not a little to the work of George Devey, whom George must have known. Unlike Devey, George's houses have substance and a sense of solid mass.

THE VICTORIAN & EDWARDIAN HOUSE

88. *Sir Ernest George (1839-1922) & Harold Peto (1884-1933)*
Poles, Hertfordshire
Design for the Drawing Room
Perspective
Insc. A Room at Poles, Herts. for E. Hanbury Esq/Ernest George & Peto Archts
Sepia pen and wash (455 x 635)
Lit. & reprd. Building News, LX, 1891, p. 669; *RIBA Catalogue... G-K*, 1973 (ed. Jill Lever),
p. 17; see also Margaret Richardson, *Architects of the Arts and Crafts Movement*, 1983, pp 59-60
RIBA DRAWINGS COLLECTION

A ROOM AT POLES, HERTS FOR E. HANBURY ESQ.   ERNEST GEORGE & PETO ARCHTS

89a

89b

The glorious and vigorously loose perspectives in coloured chalk that Wilson was so adept at producing, underline his Romantic inclinations. They have been likened to stage designs and are the most dramatic documents of the Arts and Crafts Movement. Wilson had been in the office of J.D. Sedding, an early activist of the Movement, and it was Sedding's premature death in 1891 that led to Wilson continuing his work at Welbeck for the 6th Duke of Portland. As this spectacular drawing (89) displays, Wilson's sources are in Christian and Byzantine symbols as well as Classical and Mediaeval legend, while in the Library (89a shows the 'Reading Alcove' while 89b is a view of the library) Wilson deliberately evoked Early Tudor Renaissance forms, as if to spell out in his own language the style of Robert Smythson, the celebrated Elizabethan architect, who had worked at Welbeck in the late sixteenth century. The work at Welbeck was finished in 1896 and this drawing was exhibited at the Royal Academy in 1897 when *The Builder* commented upon a 'splendid piece of colour effect'.

89. Henry Wilson (1864-1934)
Welbeck Abbey, Nottinghamshire
Design for the Chapel-Library wing
Perspective of the interior of the staircase
vestibule
Coloured chalk and watercolour (1155 x
735)
Lit. & reprd. Gavin Stamp. *The Great
Perspectivists*, 1982, p 83, pl. 91; Jill Lever
& Margaret Richardson, *The Art of the
Architect*, 1984, 25, pl.105
RIBA DRAWINGS COLLECTION

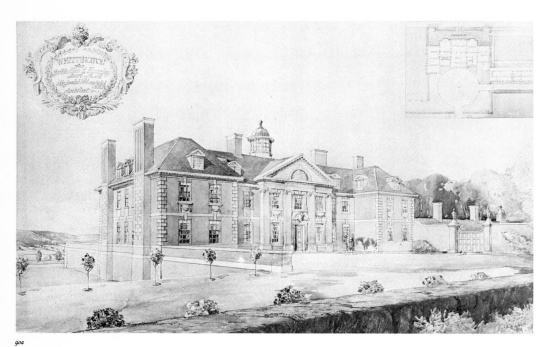

90a

Whittington (sometimes spelt without the h) is one of Blomfield's best houses in the English 'Wrenaissance' manner, designed for Sir Hudson Kearley in 1897 but not finished until 1904. However, the house that exists today although similar in style is not to this design (90). It is an astonishing fact that only five years after the first house was built Sir Hudson called in Blomfield to rebuild it once again on slightly more classical lines; hence Blomfield's later design (90a) dated 1909. In place of the late seventeenth-century style Wrenaissance porch, he substituted a Baroque stone pilaster portico of the sort often used by John James: Bloomfield's Williamite style was becoming Queen Anne Baroque.

90. Sir Reginald Blomfield (1856-1943)
Whittington, Medmenham, Buckinghamshire
Design for new house
Perspective
Insc. A House at Medmenham for Hudson Kearley Esq An 1897
Signed & dated. Reginald Blomfield Arch/97
Watercolour (280 x 560)
Lit. & reprd. The Builder, LXXXVI, 1904; Gavin Stamp, *The Great Perspectivists*, 1982 p. 85,
pl. 96 (for the later design): Richard A. Fellows, *Sir Reginald Blomfield An Edwardian Architect*,
1985, pp 60-61, pl. 37
RIBA DRAWINGS COLLECTION

91a

Hatchlands was built in 1756, but is more famous for its early interior of Robert Adam's, who came on the scene in 1759. In 1889 Halsey Ricardo had built a neo-Wren style porch to the east front, and in 1903 Blomfield added a single-story Music Room to the north side of the house (91a). It is also in Wren's style, his red brick and stone-swagged Hampton Court manner, as is this interior (91), not unlike a City Company hall or a vestry of one of Wren's City churches. Blomfield was a leading Classical revival architect, handling the Wrenaissance or the Louis style with equal facility.

91. *Sir Reginald Blomfield (1856-1943)*
Hatchlands, Surrey
Design for the Music Room
Perspective of interior, with plan and two sections
Insc. Design for New Music Room Hatchlands Guildford 1903
Signed & dated. Reginald Blomfield inv. et del 1903
Pen (510 x 560)
Lit. & reprd. The Builder, LXXXV, 1903
RIBA Drawings Collection

Plan ⅛ Scale.

Sections

·DESIGN·
·for·
·NEW·MUSIC·ROOM·
·HATCHLANDS·
·GUILDFORD·
·1903·

Ashby St Ledgers was an Elizabethan mansion notorious as the home of the Catesbys of the Gun Powder Plot. In 1903 it came into the possession of the Hon. Ivor Guest, later the 2nd Lord Wimborne, a sympathetic and intelligent client. The east front design of 1904 (92) is characteristic of Lutyens' big, pellucid wash drawings, and one can imagine him sitting in the as yet unformed garden making this design as if he were painting a watercolour view of an existing house. In fact, the south end of the front represented the end of the Elizabethan house, and in his extensions Lutyens has kept within the earlier stylistic idiom: 92a shows the east front from Lutyens' formal gardens as built.

92. *Sir Edwin Lutyens (1869-1944)*
Ashby St Ledgers, Northamptonshire
Design for remodelling the east front
Perspective elevation
Pencil, pen and wash (1000 x 530)
Lit. & reprd. RIBA Catalogue... Edwin Lutyens, ed. Margaret
Richardson, 1973, p. 12, pl. 27
RIBA DRAWINGS COLLECTION

In this sketch are encapsulated the dreams and ambitions of Julius Drewe, the wealthy founder of the Home and Colonial Stores, of building the sort of ancestral seat that might have come down through the family from a remote ancestor, Drogo de Teynon, in the thirteenth century. Lutyens was the man to do this, and he began working up rough sketches in 1909. This (93) is his first, and largest, design, for a vast castle set around a courtyard. One study on the sheet is for the castle in perspective, another shows the butressed Great Hall, and at the top is the east side, the only part to be built. Work began in 1910, was abandoned on the declaration of war in 1914, reworked to a smaller scale after the war, and not finished until 1932. This long period of gestation happily enabled Lutyens to alter and perfect his design, progressively revising the alterations and making them more sculptural. Even in its reduced form, Drogo (in 93a seen from across the gorge) is one of the most spectacular of modern castles, as well as one of the last.

Lutyens worked from graph paper, what he called his 'ideas pad', turning out pregnant drawings, sometimes given more vitality by the addition of pen and crayon, to be handed to assistants to be turned into scaled drawings. Lutyens possessed huge self-confidence, such that he would not try, or need, to charm a client by producing a highly finished, colourful drawing.

93. Sir Edwin Lutyens (1869-1954)
Castle Drogo, Devon
Sheet of preliminary perspective studies for exteriors
Pen, pencil and crayon on squared paper (405 x 530)
Lit. & reprd. Jill Lever & Margaret Richardson, *The Art of the Architect*, 1984, 120, pl. 108
RIBA DRAWINGS COLLECTION

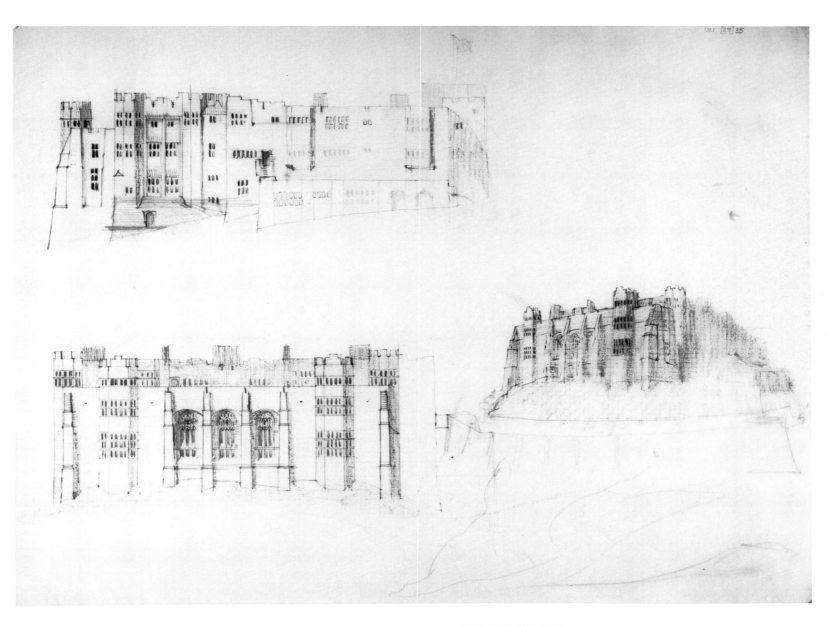

In 1918 Gordon Selfridge made a decision astonishing in the last year of the Kaiser's War, to build a vast castle on a headland called Hengistbury Head, near Bournemouth. There would have been nothing quite like it in the world, and it is tragic that it *might* have been built but was not. Tilden noted that the 'plan of the house [the large castle] was immense: it was a great and glorified dream—and so nearly realised! The only way in which I could get it all on a sheet of paper was to make to sixty-fourth scale, and then to develop it in bits.' It was to be more than 1000 feet long, had 250 bedrooms all with bathroom and dressing room, and its internal dome was only ten feet less than St Paul's Cathedral. The plan, with the north front at the bottom, is shown in *94a*, and the central rotunda in a study (*94b*). *94c* is the 'large castle' design from the north side, dated November 1919. Selfridge himself sought a new style of modern architecture, a distillation of Gothic married to the national Mediaeval castle style, and as this perspective (*94*) demonstrates, infiltrated with not a small spice of Tilden's love for Neapolitan Baroque, Sanmichele, and even Late Roman Baroque of the classical world. Compared to Hengistbury, Castle Drogo is banal. Hengistbury would have been the ideal resting place for a Citizen Kane.

With Lutyens and Oliver Hill, Tilden was perhaps one of the most successful country house architects between the wars, specialising in restoration of or additions to existing houses, and exercising great tact therein, although his taste inside his houses was 'somewhat lush and luxurious'.

94c

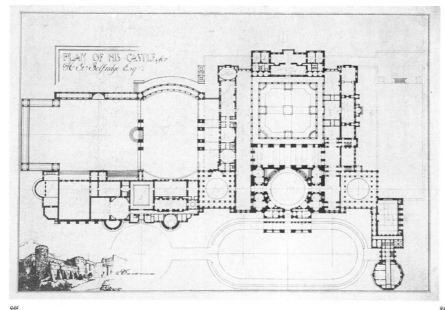

94a

94b

94. Philip Armstrong Tilden (1887-1956)
Hengistbury Head, Hampshire
Design for Gordon Selfridge's castle
View of the 'small castle' from the south
Signed & dated. November 1919 April 1920
Pen
Lit. & reprd. Philip Tilden, *True Remembrances*, 1954, ch. 4
RIBA Drawings Collection

Index of architects and houses in the Catalogue

(Names of houses & illustration numbers appear in italic)